ADAM'S RIB: MYSTERY OF THE AGES

By

James Berry

Acknowledgment

To my late devoted wife, Judith, whose love over many years gave me insight and inspiration to tell the intimate story of Christ's love for His espoused.

Contents

Introduction

Africa has many unpublicized spots of natural scenic splendor. One such site is in a remote part of the country of Sierra Leone, a country where my wife and I lived some years ago with our three children. On our way to enroll our sons in a mission boarding school far up in the interior, we left Freetown, the coastal capital city, early one morning and made our way through the small narrow streets of the crowded metropolis.

As we moved through the city, we found the market sites alongside the roadways already filled with local venders preparing for the day's street trading. We inched our way through the streets of enterprising activity toward the nearby beautiful cerulean estuary of the Sierra Leone River where a renowned sea captain sailed his slave ship to pick up human cargo for plantations across the Atlantic. We know him today as Captain John Newton, slaver-turned-clergyman, and friend of Wilberforce, the English parliamentarian who caused the enactment of laws prohibiting the institution of slavery within the British Empire. Around the world, Newton's notoriety comes more from his songwriting than his job as a slaver—"Amazing Grace" is his best-known hymn.

First, the Portuguese sailed here to expand and establish their interest in trade. They built a fort on this river as a base to exploit the natural resources, then resorted to the most lucrative of all resources: the taking and selling of humanity. It was one of many forts they built on the west coast of Africa in their attempt to dominate and protect their trade in human life. After the Portuguese, there came more ships from other countries sailing the river in search of helpless victims. The ruins of the fort that lay under the tropical overgrowth were at one time a fortress used as a prison for slaves before they were forced to board ships for another world.

As my family and I drove on, we could not see the historical pain on the surface of the topographical beauty the river itself flowed through. The velvet-covered tropical terrain and the sudden ascending majestic mountains showed the marks of nature's ability to cover up the scars of the past. In spite of the beautiful overlay of tropical forest, we knew that there was a story here of pain that needed to be heard in every new generation. It occurred to me as we moved on down the narrow road on our journey to the mission school that perhaps nature itself was the first teacher in the art of cosmetology. Nature had done this for herself here in this land scarred with historical pain.

The longer we drove up into the interior away from the coast, the narrower the roads became. Two walls of green jungle lined each side of the red lateritic roadway. Natural beauty, wildlife, and small villages with mud houses stood out at us as if they were on a stage performing for our benefit. Our sons were entertained with monkeys swinging and frolicking in trees and scenes of other wildlife in natural habitat. Active uninhibited nature was entertainment for our sons—better than any electronic device on the market today.

After driving several hours over rugged, dusty, and sometimes muddy roads there suddenly appeared a brief opening in the wall of the tropical forest. Through that clearing, miles off in the distance, we saw a cluster of mountain rock formations that created the outline of the upper part of a camel. The scene was spectacular and seemed to come from nowhere, and like a phantasmagoric appearance, it emerged but for a few minutes. As we drove on, the configuration of a camel faded; the window of opportunity for observing it was short-lived. When we saw it for the first time on this trip, we were awestruck at the site. We later learned that people called it "Camelback Mountain."

Our experiences of seeing camels in zoos and studying about them in books permitted us to identify what nature was showing us in geological formations. Were it not for our knowledge of this unique-looking creature, the mountain-shaped outline of the likeness of a camel would have passed us by. Three things gave life to what we saw: knowledge, perception, and distance. On that day, distance created the view; it was a memorable event. The villagers living in the foothills of Camelback Mountain never saw the camel-like features; it required distance.

Since that day of discovering the outline of a camel in the tropics of Africa, I have thought of how distance from early creation allows us to see broader, clearer outlines of biblical truth. Jesus said, "Every scribe which is instructed unto the kingdom of heaven is like a man that is an householder, which bringeth forth out of his treasures things "new and old" (Matt. 13:52 KJV). The incarnate Deity of the Anointed-One, His death, resurrection, and ascension are the new treasures on display within the household of the informed scribe. The New Covenant writers polished those new treasure-truths with great luster and permanence. As scribes instructed in matters of the Kingdom of Heaven, the believer can use these new treasures as a telescope to look back into the distant past to find the old, faraway hidden counterpart-treasures under the dust of overlooked events that speak of matters that transcend our known world. One of these old treasures set in stone is the story of Adam and his rib, a love story that flows through Scripture like an artery that carries life to the body, a monumental event in history that shows God's centerpiece in His dealings with man.

The monogamous institution of marriage in Eden was the creation of a natural law that God would use to show His love for humankind. Every civilization since Eden has registered the inherent drive to codify in written or unwritten form the role of marriage in society. Like the migratory birds that know to take their flights to the north and south at the right times of the year, humans have an inner sense to give acceptance and legal status to the role of this institution. The Apostle Paul makes clear a common axiom in Romans 1:20: "The invisible things of God from the creation of the world are clearly seen, being understood by the things that are made."

Marriage is an institution that is intended to show God's nature and purpose for the human race. It comes packaged as a unit of three parts: the first being the Garden of Eden event with Adam and Eve; the second, the bonding union between Israel and God; and the third and final, the one of mystery, Christ and His espoused. God gave us the first marriage as a pattern to understand the latter two.

When the householder takes this old treasure that tells the greatest love story ever, he holds it in his hands with a white-knuckled grip because of its value in showing a three-dimensional picture of how God has dealt with man. Adam's rib is a picture-within-a-picture that needs to be told, a marriage that reaches all the way from Eden in Genesis to the Revelation in heaven. The saga carries all the drama of a stage production where in the end good conquers evil and the protagonist gets the girl he loves.

Sometimes we overlook the part of life that is closest to us, and in our age of disappointment, hurt, and failure in the institution of marriage we can easily lose sight of the higher and more noble picture of what God intended for us to see in the Edenic monogamous union of two people. Adam's Rib: Mystery of the Ages is a series of creative, thematic biblical expositions on the theme of love and marriage and its transcendent truth of man's union with God through His Son, Jesus.

Chapter 1

The First DNA Donor

Today, our distance in history from early times allows science to show a broader view of one of the oldest biblical treasures: the picture of Christ and the church in the creation of the first man and woman. Until the twentieth century, it was hidden, a treasure from the past, waiting to be brought out, polished, and put on display in the age of modern science. The outside cover of the treasure box reads:

> And Jehovah God causeth a deep sleep to fall upon the man, and he sleepeth, and He taketh one of his ribs, and closeth up flesh in its stead. And Jehovah God buildeth up the rib which He hath taken out of the man into a woman, and bringeth her in unto the man; and the man saith, This [is] the [proper] step! bone of my bone, and flesh of my flesh! for this it is called Woman, for from a man hath this been taken. (Gen. 2:21-23 Young's Literal Translation)

Unlike a suspenseful novel in which one waits until the last chapter to see what happens, the Bible introduces us to the oldest recorded central theme, purpose, and outcome of God's drama with man by giving us, in hidden picture form, the end of the story at the beginning of the Book. The fullest meaning of this age-old treasure lay silent in Holy Script until the modern age of the electron microscope and inquisitive minds. The birth of the church, the mystical Body of Christ, as recorded in the New Testament, the last chapter of the book, was the finished product of what was pictured in shadow-form in the book of Genesis in the creation of Adam and Eve.

Fortunately, for us living today, scientific research has opened a window of knowledge to reveal the fullest meaning of why God chose to make man and his complementary opposite gender in the manner and time-sequence that He did.

In 1953, two research scientists, British-born Francis Crick and James Watson, an American, discovered the spiral double-helix structure of deoxyribonucleic acid (DNA). At the time of this discovery, the world was unaware of the extent of the power and influence this sleeping giant would have on society in matters of law enforcement and genetic engineering. Also, little did the church know how this research discovery would give light on the theme of God's pattern for two creations: one at the beginning of man's history—the other at the end.

When we used to study earth science and astronomy, it gave us a sense of wonderment seeing God's design and order in the creation of matter; however, modern genetic research has exploded exponentially the argument of design in creation by what science has found in one single human cell. When God created the first pair of the human species, He did not create the male and female at the same time:

And the Lord God took the man, and put him into the garden of Eden to dress it and to keep it....And the Lord God said, It is not good that the man should be alone; I will make him an help meet for him. (Gen. 2:15, 18 KJV)

The pause of time between Adam and Eve's creation shows a significant chronological arrangement in history: first Adam, then Eve. Not only were Adam and Eve created at two different intervals, they were created in two different ways. First, Adam was formed, then "God breathed His breath into him, and he became a living soul" (Gen. 2:7). In the next stage of human creation, after a lapse of time, God caused a deep sleep to come over Adam, and from his rib cage, He took genetic bone material (DNA), then used the raw material to form Eve, Adam's future wife. The ancient text, according to Robert Young's nineteenth century word-for-word literal Hebrew translation, describes Eve's creation:

Jehovah God buildeth up the rib which He hath taken out of the man into a woman, and bringeth her in unto the man. (Gen. 2:21 Young's Literal Translation)

God chose to create His first two humans in a way that would picture what awaited the human race in the fullness of time. Subsequent to Eve's emergence as a newly created person from Adam's rib material, there was a formal introduction of the two, at which time Adam responded by proclaiming, "She is bone of my bones and flesh of my flesh" (Gen. 2:23 KJV). Adam acknowledged that Eve's physical body came from his removed DNA bone material. God did not choose to duplicate the process of Adam's creation in the making of Eve, his wife-to-be, the results of which would have made two DNA gene pools. Thus, from this biblical scene and record, it could be argued that there existed only one DNA gene source for the whole human race, and its origin was in one single person: the first-created human, the man Adam. There were two separate human creations but one gene pool. Eve would produce issue, and pass on to the human race only the DNA that came from her donor.

From afar in our age of science, we see this picture of the Genesis creation of Adam and Eve as a long shadow cast across the pages of history pointing to another Donor and new creation. Old and new treasures come together at Calvary when the rib cage of the second Adam is incised, and there flows from His body a new higher spiritual order that will give life to the second Eve, the church, His mystical bride.

When the second Adam said on the cross, "It is finished," the life of the espoused began to take on form, and on the day of Pentecost, the donor-recipient took her first neonatal breath. In that upper room where the building shook with the wind of the breath of God, the creative genetic transfer of life was finalized, and from that day forward, she began making herself ready for the grand event of the royal marriage to her Donor, whom having not seen, she loved.

Today, while the espoused waits for the sound of the

wedding appointment, she acknowledges that her life, and everything she is, comes from her Donor's DNA. She affirms that her body is created from His and that there is no life in and of herself apart from him; cell growth and replication in her mystical body will be the result of His gift of life. She will bear His image and carry in her body all the DNA components of her Donor. The rite of the Passover of Holy Communion, a memorial of His body and blood, will be her tangible reminder that she is made from Him, and her creation comes only from His body. Isaiah reminds the nation of Israel of this event: "Yet it pleased the Lord to bruise him...he shall see his seed..." (Isaiah 53:10 KJV).

In this late hour of God's time clock for man, an old hidden treasure has been dusted off with modern scientific DNA research. Its veracity has turned on a great floodlight that amplifies a steganographic message: that the underlying truth in the Genesis human creation is an earthly prototype of a greater mystical creation to follow. As Adam is shown to be the first and only original genetic donor for his bride-to-be, even so Christ, the second Adam, offers His body as donor-material for the creation of a new and living way. This new mystical body-creation of a higher order two thousand years ago commences the waiting period for the promise of His return and the anticipated marriage celebration. Today, late in the night of the account of man, this old treasure is uncovered and put on display as the Donor-recipient burns her lamp filled with oil and keeps herself prepared for the midnight arrival of her life-giving Benefactor.

Time has seasoned this hidden truth, and the great Householder has polished it well for our scientific age. The Apostle John reminds us that God will soon bring the Donor and recipient together for a face-to-face meeting: "The marriage of the Lamb is come, and his wife hath made herself ready" (Rev. 19:7 KJV).

Chapter 2

Another Steganographic DNA Story

> Why speakest thou unto them in parables? He
> answered and said unto them, because it is given
> unto you to know the mysteries of the kingdom of
> heaven, but to them it is not given. Therefore
> speak I to them in parables, because they seeing,
> see not; and hearing, they hear not, neither do they
> understand. (Matt. 13:10, 11, 13 KJV)

Steganography is a method used to hide secret messages and comes from the Greek meaning covered writing. Its use in passing on secret messages dates back to 440 B.C., when Herodotus, the Greek historian, cites an example: "Demeratus sent a warning about a forthcoming attack on Greece by writing it on a wooden panel and covering it in wax." Another ancient example is that of Histiaeus, who shaved the head of his most trusted slave and tattooed a message on it. After his hair had grown, it concealed the message. When the slave reached his destination, the removal of his hair revealed the intent of instigating a revolt against the Persians. In modern times, steganography has taken on very sophisticated methods of concealing messages.

It was in World War II that the American military used the Navajo language for coded messages in the war with Japan. Marines recruited Navajos to learn a code using their own spoken language that would serve to help win the war in the South Pacific. The Navajo language, unwritten and spoken only in the States, became an effective tool. Those who used the language to send secret messages were known as the Code Talkers, and throughout the war, the Japanese failed to break the Navajo code.

The Bible is another source of steganographically hidden messages of a different order intended to be understood by those whose hearts have been enlightened to truth. Luke records Jesus saying, "I thank thee, O Father, Lord of heaven and earth, that thou hast hidden these things from the wise and prudent, and hast revealed them unto babes" (Luke 10:21 KJV). Uncovering hidden treasure truths in the Scriptures require more than formal learning and human experience. They come only from inner perception through faith. Biblical knowledge acquired merely through rote learning without faith remains hidden and unproductive. In Jesus' day, the rabbinical schools were full of learned scholars of the Scriptures, but few came forward to give affirmation to the One who was the embodiment of Truth. Complete clarity of truth occurs when biblical knowledge is perceived by faith in the human spirit.

In ancient times, when the nation of Israel struggled with its northern nemesis, Syria, the great prophet Elisha was a constant informer of Syria's planned military actions. To thwart Elisha's continued disruption of the king's border raids against Israel, the king of Syria sent a large contingent of soldiers to the city of Dothan where Elisha was staying. Early in the morning after the Syrian forces had surrounded the city, Elisha's companion went out early and saw the hopeless circumstances they were in. In desperation, the young friend said to Elisha, "What shall we do?" Elisha then prayed for a second pair of eyes for his friend: "Lord, I pray thee, open his eyes that he may see. And the Lord opened the eyes of the young man; and he saw: and, behold, the mountain was full of horses and chariots of fire round about" (2 Kings 6:17 KJV).

In spiritual matters, it is the set of eyes that see beyond the human experience that brings to life hidden images that tell the silent story of a thousand words. Jesus painted many of these pictures in the minds of his disciples in the form of parables, and sometimes they were drawn by his own hands in acts of miracles that had veiled truth that reached beyond the miracle itself. Such was the case when He used His spittle, mixed with the dust-of-earth, to bring sight to a man who had been born blind:

> When He had thus spoken, he spat on the ground, and made clay of the spittle, and He anointed the eyes of the blind man with the clay and said unto him, go wash in the pool of Siloam. He went his way therefore, and washed, and came seeing. (John 9:6-7 KJV)

Jesus healed many blind people in His earthly Messianic ministry showing Himself to be the Promised

One. However, there is only one recorded event in the New Testament where he healed a man born blind by mixing His spittle with dust-of-earth and applying it as clay to the eyes of one born sightless. This leaves us with a challenge to look beyond what we see in this miracle to discover a treasure of hidden truth.

If we derive truth from the stories Jesus told of the prodigal son, the woman who lost the ten pieces of silver, or the one lost sheep, then we must elicit insight from this record of Jesus healing the man born blind. In this event, Jesus acted out the story of the gospel in the way He healed the man born blind, leaving us emblematic truth that defined God's love for the human race.

Every living person carries his own unique DNA code. There are no two people on the face of the earth who have the same DNA, except identical twins, which are a result of a fertilized egg dividing itself into two persons. Even identical twins have different fingerprints, which allow for some specific identifiable marks between them. Each cell in the human body carries a universe so infinite that science still shocks the world at its findings. Research inside the human cell is an ongoing process with new discoveries coming in every day.

The uniqueness of every living person is reinforced when Jesus said, "Even the very hairs of your head are all numbered" (Luke 12:7 KJV). In the disciples' day, the Lord used the best analogy possible to show God's personal concerns with individuality. He not only makes every person special as an individual, He even creates a record-keeping system for the hairs on the scalp. David, in the Old Testament, expressed God's omniscience: "My substance was not hid from thee, when I was made in secret" (Psa. 139:15 KJV). The newborn's inimitable genetic profile reflects God's ability to know each person who comes into life in an all-knowing way. When we were born, each of us was given a name by ancestry and parental choice, but there was another identity given at the time of conception in the form of our DNA.

All normal cells in the human body have forty-six chromosomes. There is one exception: the reproductive cell carries only twenty-three chromosomes. When fertilization occurs in an egg, each parent will have contributed 50 percent of the DNA components in the offspring. Mary, the chosen young Jewish peasant virgin, gave twenty-three of her human chromosomes as a participant in the transference of Deity into human embryonic form; science fails to lead us further into this great mystery. Thus, God chose the obstacle course of simple faith to believe what science cannot measure: that He gave the other twenty-three genetic components to create a normal healthy baby boy who was all God and all man.

Today, the study of DNA and its use in forensic identification has caused the creation of collection banks that are burgeoning into an ongoing industry in this country. DNA storage systems presently used are making the samples available for a later date. Suggested viable DNA samples are taken from:

Saliva (first choice)

Blood (second choice)
Hair strands (10-20 with follicles still attached)
Skin samples
Finger or toenail
Tooth

Saliva is the first choice in the DNA sample collection list. From the New Testament record of Jesus healing the man born blind, we see Him using His DNA in saliva mixed with dust-of-earth to form a clay-paste for anointing the blind eyes. Whereas much of the Lord's teaching comes in the form of stories and parables intended for immediate use and understanding, He chooses to demonstrate by acting-out in silent picture-form a message of truth for us living afar off in our age of science. By mixing His DNA in saliva with the dust from the earth, He shows a picture beyond the miracle itself.

His spittle carried His DNA identity. If Jesus were living today, unbelievers in genetic research would demand a DNA saliva sample in an attempt to disprove His claim to Deity. They would be an extension of His critics during His earthly time: "Others, tempting him, sought of him a sign from heaven" (Luke 11:16 KJV).

As the disciples watched with the crowd pressed in closely around Jesus and the blind man, He knelt and blended together His spittle with the soil of earth, soil over which the masses of human traffic had trodden for centuries. He crushed together the two parts to form a clay paste, then applied it to the eyes of a person who had never seen the beauty of life, nature, or members of his own family. Earth mixed with His saliva, applied to the eyes of darkness, spoke to what He had become: God made in human form, crushed to give light to them who sat in darkness.

God chose to mix Himself with the human race by meeting His creation halfway. He took what He had made from the dust of earth, the virgin Mary's 23 chromosomes, blended Himself with that creation and became what His creation was, so eyes of blindness could be healed: "But when the fullness of time was come, God sent forth His son made of a woman" (Gal. 4:4 KJV).

Dust of earth in the hands of Jesus addresses Adam's physical creation. Dust of earth blended with His saliva by His own hands shows Deity shrouded with humanity bringing sight to those who are born blind. He is the principal agent, choosing to form Himself with man's dust nature. The pulverized clay in His own hands used to anoint blind eyes encapsulated Isaiah's description of what He became: "His appearance was so disfigured beyond that of any man and his form marred beyond human likeness" (Isa. 52:14 NIV). Jesus was disfigured upon a cross of pain but shrouded with heaven's majesty.

When He said, "It is finished," He invited the world that had been born blind to wash in the water held by the clay basin of His humanity. Zechariah saw the scene that would bring sight to blindness: "In that day there shall be a fountain opened to the house of David and to the inhabitants of Jerusalem for sin and for uncleanness" (Zech. 13:1 KJV). When His body was offered up, water flowed from it: "One of the soldiers with a spear pierced his side, and forthwith came out blood and water" (John. 19:34 KJV). History shows that millions upon millions have made the journey to the fountain of clay holding the water of life.

When God planned the wedding event for His Son at the foundation of the world, He sought a suitable bride with one qualifying standard for the prospective wife: she had to be one with perfect eyesight. There is no chamber of darkness greater than the legal status sin confines man to. It is among the blind of earth that the Son pursues His bride, and the adjudication of that legal guilt of blindness is processed through the court of God's love by His Son's gift of eyesight through His bruised and crushed body on Calvary.

The act of Jesus making clay with His spittle was recorded only once in His earthly ministry. It was neither repeated by Him nor practiced among His disciples in the early church. The reinforcement of its meaning by the avoidance of its repetition shows the truth and clarity of Scripture: "So Christ was once offered to bear the sins of many" (Heb. 9:28 KJV).

Earth and saliva mixed together to form clay expressed God in human form. What defined the dissimilarity of this clay from any other was the DNA it contained. From afar, in our age of science, we can use the new discovery of DNA as a polishing cloth to bring out the luster of an old treasure of hidden truth by understanding why Jesus used the method He did to bring sight to blindness.

Chapter 3

Love Is a Creation

When I was young and attending a university, it wasn't too long after the epic discovery of the DNA double helix by Francis Crick and James Watson. In my early days, DNA research was still in its infancy. I was enrolled in a class studying human genetics and had the assignment of doing a lab test with an advanced microscope. The objective was to use the male and female reproductive cells from marine sea urchins to simulate human genetic fertilization.

After successfully extracting genetic reproductive cells from a male and female sea urchin, one egg was isolated on a slide under the microscope. Sea urchin sperm were then added to the slide. The life one sees under a microscope is another world: a universe that mirrors the majesty of God's creation. The single sea urchin egg I had placed on the slide remained still, lifeless like a statue. The reproductive cells from the male, like a magnet, swam in its direction. Only one of the swimming cells entered the egg, then, as if a barrier were put up, it excluded all others. The egg remained motionless. I continued to observe the process under the microscope, when suddenly, change happened: the egg that once looked lifeless, that had allowed the entry of one male genetic cell, started to quiver. Before my eyes the two single cells that had bonded into one, each having contributed to the union an equal number of DNA chromosomes, suddenly replicated into two conjoined cells, then, a few minutes later, divided into four cells. Timed at exact intervals, it continued quivering, replicating exponentially new cells in the development of a sea urchin. That day in the lab when two cells became one, I saw the creation of life, the beginning of a new living organism.

When I took my eyes from the microscope to write my report, my naked eye could no longer see the newly started life on the slide that was still quivering, creating new cells from its DNA messaging center. I had visited a microscopic world and participated in a picture of the conception of life from two opposite genetic cells of the same species—picture images that would stay with me for as long as I lived.

Since those early days, I have looked through the microscope of a higher order to understand the miracle of two opposites becoming one: the biblical record of the creation of the first man and woman in a marriage union. The order of the original creation of man shows that God first makes Adam, and from Adam He creates Eve, the second party, then finishes His creation by reversing the order: taking the two separate human opposite entities and rejoining them back into one—the marriage union. With the creation of the marriage institution, one might say that God defies the mathematical law of natural order by making two equal one. What we do know is that when

He joins the two opposites of His creation, an image of mystery becomes swathed with a law of love.

When God's breath entered man at his creation, he became a living being with a law of love that would govern the institution of oneness in marriage until the end of time. This is why romance and the union of marriage has a certain hidden mystery with a force of energy that defies human understanding—it transcends all instinctual and chemically driven human appetites and becomes the regenerative force that keeps on building the inner life of a marriage union—even through senescent years. An elderly father, who had lost his lifelong spouse, was asked by his son, "Dad, how old do you think Mom will be when you see her again?" The father's immediate response was, "It doesn't matter—it's who she is that counts." This is the mystique of a marriage union—a relationship of two becoming one over the single rail of the law of love, with age only serving to sweeten the journey.

When David says by inspiration, "I am fearfully and wonderfully made" (Ps. 139:14 KJV), he taps on the front door of God's centerpiece of human life: the ability to receive and give love, the inexplicable creation of the deepest and most profound emotion. That energy is put into the most intimate expressions in the Song of Solomon and is characterized with one verse: "Many waters cannot quench love, nor can floods drown it" (8:4 KJV). Down through the ages, others have penned the intrigue of the mystique of love. The sage of early English drama, playwright William Shakespeare, knew the intrinsic value of love in human interactions. He placed it in public view by creating classical works of literature that embellished the part of a person that went beyond physiology, intelligence, and sometimes rationality. He used what had always been part of the human experience: the intrigue of love. It was on his strings of drama he played the music of love, the mysterious part of the soul.

In the beginning, God made man as a complex being in His own image. The heart of that creation was not his higher intelligence alone, which he had above all other species, but a combination of three parts: mind, will, and emotion. Some call these three parts the essence of the soul, and whether there is agreement on this or not, all will concur that these are the forces that make up the complexity of man and give distinct individuality. However, three can sometimes create conflict.

There is a reason people use the expression, "Three is a crowd." What gives meaning to this is when we observe three six-year-old children at play instead of just two. The presence of three children can sometimes give rise to the exclusion of one from the other two. Two has symmetrical balance for harmony in relationships. After all, didn't God make only one wife and one husband for both genders in original creation?

Among the things our ancestors took with them from the Garden in Genesis were animal skins for clothing, a conscience knowing good and evil, and that "three's-a-crowd" thing. Since the garden expulsion, the animal skins have been discarded, but the three parts, mind, will, and emotion, are still with us, and not far behind is the tagalong voice of the human conscience. These are the driving forces for man's good and bad outcomes. Today, our struggles are not with the question of why God makes us so complicated with these different parts, but rather how they are to be arranged and balanced to make life work for us.

When I was a kid on the playground, I was always the active child. One of my favorite feats was to walk on top of the seesaw, stand in the middle, and shift my weight to balance the board as level as I could. Making it equal was the challenge for me, not sitting on one end with someone else on the other side. By standing on top, I had the power to make it go either way I wanted all by myself—it made me feel like I was in control. Since then, I have reflected on this experience being something like what God planned for the delicate balance needed in the three-part system we have inside of us. The will part of us is forever destined to be the balancer at the control center at the top of the board with reason and emotion sitting at each end of the seesaw. Both ends of the board are always subject to the will—the person at the top of the seesaw—the will-balancer. However, for the whole person to live in balance, all three compartments must flow together under the command of the will over which the conscience serves as an arbitrator. We all know people who have allowed their wills to lean too heavily on the seesaw board of life toward emotions. They live with an outlook that everything's about self, seeking the acceptance of the wrong people, allowing the senses to be titillated with material things, and wrong pleasures.

The mind, the other end of the seesaw, the processor that handles information and cognitive thought, is sometimes the heavyweight on that board and goes undetected as a guilty party because of the value placed on intelligence and rational thought. Sometimes I wish my computer had feelings so it would know how I felt when trying to find pathways for solutions with certain technical issues. But it doesn't. It's loaded with information; it knows everything, except how I feel. The only way I get a response from it is to give it more information by typing on the keyboard, and sometimes that doesn't help because my knowledge is limited.

The mind part of us can sometimes act like an unfeeling, detached computer filled with knowledge, has answers for everything, yet cannot cross the line and allow feelings to influence what is known. Too much weight at this end of the board can cause disengagement and detachment in relationships.

The mind and emotion ends of the seesaw are not entities in themselves; they are merely used by the person in charge at the top of the board—the free will. This complicated tripartite creation inside man, the "three's-a-crowd" trilogy, was perhaps what David made reference to in our being "fearfully made." One doesn't have to go to a circus to see a tightrope performance high over the spectators to understand the need for balance—everyday life is the challenge.

When balance happens in life, these three parts, the mind, will, and emotion, act like gears that move in synchronized motion in response to the human conscience, each meshing together for a single operation. If precision balance is required to make life run with optimal smoothness for one person, then consider the complications when one's three-compartment system is juxtaposed and integrated with another opposite-gendered individual in the union of marriage.

Now comes the mystery of marriage. If one gender carries three internal complex working parts, the mind, will, and emotion, and marries, it gives the marriage union a configuration of six working parts that must be orchestrated for harmony. The balancing board now has two wills at the top attempting to govern one set of emotions on one end and another set of intellects at the other. Under natural order, this balancing act appears doomed from the start—a paradox—an oxymoronic union. How do three different independent parts that are combined with another three autonomous parts blend together to make one working organism? It takes a miracle of God's creation—love—and it all comes packaged together from the garden scene when God put part of Himself inside the species of man.

Love, in its broad generic form, is a creation of God that is demonstrated when acted upon in the recesses of the human conscience, the part of man that inherently knows the difference between good and evil. This is the glue that holds human societies together and produces different levels of love with varying intensities.

However, the marriage union falls under a special category outside the broader picture of love. It is a mystical union where two combine who and what they are into one single unit, each contributing 50 percent to the newly formed marriage cell, and unlike the natural law where cell replication in the human body reaches the tipping point and enters the stage of senescence, the marriage union thrives with age and time.

Successful marriage relationships are mysterious because they somehow continue to work in spite of those six different parts of diversity in the union. The power of His created love provides the oil for smooth operations inside the marriage union. The mystery it holds mirrors Christ's love for His espoused and what awaits the faithful in the world to come.

"A man shall leave his father and his
mother, and shall cleave unto his wife:
and they shall be one flesh."

Chapter 4

Abraham's Sand-and-Star Descendants

Now when I passed by you, and looked upon you, behold, your time was the time of love; and I spread my skirt over you, and covered your nakedness: yea, I swore unto you, and entered into a covenant with you, says the Lord Jehovah, and you became mine. (Ezekiel 16:8)

The record of the first marriage union in Eden shows the institution as the major part of the way God will deal with His creation. The principle of two becoming one through the mystical creation of love will be the prototype of what will follow in two future marriages of a higher order: God as the husband to Israel, and Christ as the Bridegroom to the church. The latter two marriages are put in motion when God courts Abraham with certain dowry promises of geography and posterity as numerous as the sand upon the seashore and the stars of the heavens.

Treasures sometimes have two sides with one story. Henry the Navigator did for the fifteenth century Age of Exploration what England did for the Industrial

Revolution more than two centuries later. In the fifteenth century, the king of Portugal advanced his country ahead of other European nations by his expansion of Portugal's interest in maritime trade and discovery. In search of a new trade route to the East for commerce in spices, the many pelagic voyages by the Portuguese led Vasco da Gama to find the cape of South Africa, opening the door to the wealth of spices in the East. This newly found water route around South Africa brought prosperity to Portugal and heralded de Gama as a national hero and celebrity. Everyone believed at the time that he was the first to find this new water route; however, there was an older face and another side to the story.

When archaeologists excavated ancient Egyptian tombs more than two hundred years after da Gama, they found cuneiform writings detailing the very route around the Cape that the Portuguese captain had discovered. Da Gama was not the first to find that ocean passage to the East. It was a well-known trade route among people living in the Mediterranean area two thousand years before da Gama's time. Up until the discovery of the deciphered writings inside the tombs of Egypt, Europeans thought the passage around the Cape had only one face to it, and it belonged to da Gama. However, these writings on ancient walls of stone revealed another story in another period in time. The record of history had been rediscovered.

On May 14, 1948, the international community in the United Nations approved the creation of the modern nation of Israel. Most of the nations voting in favor of Israel's birth into nationhood came from those influenced by the many pogroms of the nineteenth century and the Holocaust under Adolf Hitler during World War II. Few, if any, had a truly historical biblical perspective of the people whom they were rearranging on the globe. However, those who had read the ancient Hebrew Script were well aware that ships had sailed this passage long before 1948. The world today sees Israel floating on a turbulent raging sea as a Gordian knot in a Middle East conflict. Underneath the floating nation of Israel there is a long anchor reaching back almost four thousand years. Like the Cape of South Africa, a known passageway to the East by the ancients, but unknown to Europe in her Age of Exploration, Israel was a nation long before the twentieth century. Ships of history had sailed this passage before 1948.

It is our descent to the bottom of these turbulent seas into the depths of where Israel's anchor rests that we discover why she is a modern nation today. It is also there that we find the marriage arrangements God made with Israel. While the new treasure floats on top of the violent surface, the lost knowledge of her past lies below the surface. Let us descend to the end of the anchor-line that holds her in place, and look at the steps God took to create the nation that floats on top of the ocean floor.

The Bible is a love story and begins with the introduction of a marriage in Eden between two opposite genders: one man and one woman. It is a picture of two becoming one with the commission to procreate.

This principle of two becoming one is elevated to a higher level when God chooses to bond with a people who will give birth to His own offspring. It begins with one man by the name of Abram who lived in Ur, part of a region of the Fertile Crescent, the cradle of civilization.

Nearby Ur was the life-producing artery of the Euphrates River that ran seventeen hundred miles from its source, emptying into the Persian Gulf creating life and wealth for the inhabitants it touched. It was in this region that God intervened in the affairs of men by appearing to Abram with the command to leave his country and go to a land of promise. He migrated with his family six hundred miles northward up the Mesopotamian valley to a site called Haran. It was there that God renewed His promise of making him a blessing to the world, and from that moment on Abram was destined to become a wandering nomadic nobleman of great wealth and influence:

> Get thee out of thy country, and from thy kindred, and from thy father's house, unto a land that I will show thee: And I will make of thee a great nation, and I will bless thee, and make thy name great; and thou shalt be a blessing: And I will bless them that bless thee, and curse him that curseth thee: and in thee shall all families of the earth be blessed. (Gen. 12:1-2 KJV)

God's first communication to Abram concerned him, his descendants, and other families on the earth. Emphasis was made in this promise to include families outside his own. After his arrival in his new land of

Canaan there was reaffirmation of the original covenant. This time it came with more details:

> Lift up now thine eyes, and look from the place where thou art northward, and southward, and eastward, and westward: For all the land which thou seest, to thee will I give it, and to thy seed for ever. (Gen. 13:14-15 KJV)

This prophetic communication to Abram carried with it the promise of geography and far-reaching longevity. It was a marriage proposal to him and his seed and would be legally consummated at Sinai with the giving of the Law and Commandments. During Abram's nomadic journeys in Canaan, God changed his name to Abraham and appeared to him from time-to-time to buttress His first encounter at Haran. God's last reminder of his covenant with Abraham was at Mount Moriah, after his test of offering Isaac, his miracle son, as a sacrifice:

> I will bless thee, and in multiplying I will multiply thy seed as the stars of the heaven, and as the sand which is upon the sea shore; and thy seed shall possess the gate of his enemies. And In thy seed shall all the nations of the earth be blessed. (Gen. 22:17-18 KJV)

When God promised Abraham that his seed would be as numerous as the sand on the seashore and the stars of the sky, He spoke in hyperbolic form to emphasize his numerical posterity. He also alluded to two different types of descendants: sand, being the prolificacy of his offspring with physical boundaries in Canaan, which would later be taken and occupied by his millions of descendants, and the stars, a mystical innumerable people representing what would later become known as the church, the "families of earth," which would include both Jews and Gentiles.

THE SAND KINGDOM

When God used the analogy of sand on the seashore to describe the prolificacy of Abraham's seed, He also gave us a picture describing certain characteristics that would follow his descendants. Sand was a very unstable geological material. Abraham's offspring were destined, not only to be as numerous as the sand on the seashore, but would also reflect sand's inherent instability by leaving a history of broken laws and polytheistic alliances. Her failures would be matched only the grains of sand that numbered her. However, sand, a major component in the building industry in modern times, when mixed with cement and crushed stone, becomes strength. God will take the weakness of Abraham's sand descendants and turn them into a viable nation.

Several hundred years after Abraham's descendents went down to Egypt to escape the drought and famine in Canaan, his offspring found themselves on a sterile uninhabitable remote desert in great numbers. Freed from the bondage of slavery in Egypt, they looked to the leadership of a man who was formerly a political insider in the courts of Pharaoh, king of Egypt.

Having been delivered from slavery, Abraham's descendants were without a country, lacking any sense of national unity. Potential disaster awaited these now migratory sand-people on a vast arid wasteland; they were primitive and culturally tied to their background of bondage in Egypt, the place of their birth. They lacked a sense of belonging to the bigger picture of a political whole and at the same time were displaying another part of their sand nature. While Moses was on Mount Sinai receiving the Magna Charta of his day for a new nation, Abraham's people were on the desert floor frolicking in the sand, the same unstable substance they were. Though they were devoid of any patriotic nationhood and bore the loss of any security of even being slaves, God chose to do more than just increase the number of Abraham's sand descendants. He would take them, using the heat of isolation on the desert to coalesce a people into a viable nation of perpetuity.

The greatest influence on the development of Western Society, apart from the Christian faith, came through the Roman Empire. Rome possessed cleverness at borrowing what other people knew and developed. She was pragmatic and incorporated what worked into her own system. One thing characterized Rome: uniformity. She had uniform laws, standard languages of Greek and Latin, uniform construction, and common economic systems. This uniformity gave Rome what she needed to build and sustain a far-reaching diverse Empire.

However, long before the Roman Empire's great arm of uniformity were God's civic and religious laws that bound together a loosely knitted sand-people.

The story of forging a needed uniformity of laws over a backward people began at the top of a mountain where God met a man and gave him a religious system of law and order that would act as glue with which to build nationhood. These religious and civic laws came with great signs and wonders. The results of that dramatic scene of earth-shaking events on the desert floor continue to this day.

The introduction of the Law and Commandments, with a system of worship that revealed the one true God, gave the newly formed mass of sand-people the needed tools to build a nation destined to cover a large geographical region. God's purpose for Israel was to become a national womb. She would conceive and give birth to a promised Messiah, an Offspring of Israel, who would provide Abraham a new generation of star-descendants of the families of earth. The nationhood of Israel, in embryonic form, was cast upon everything dead and lifeless: the desert was barren, and the people God was giving life to were void of any redeeming cultural and social standing. However, in this deadness God brought life to Israel with the mixture of soft clay in the form of law and a religious system of worship. Time, in the heat of the desert, would harden these people into a vessel with qualities that would carry the voices of truth
down through the ages.

Abraham's descendants through Isaac are called

Jews. Jews are distinct and measurable by ethnicity and religion. Today, the best answer to the atheist who asks for proof of the existence of God is merely the simple reply, "The Jewish people and the nation of modern Israel." From the time of Moses in the bulrushes, through the twentieth century, there has never been a people who has suffered at the hands of organized attempts of genocide as the sand-people. They have defied all laws of mathematical and historical probability, and after three millennia, they possess a national identity along with the same Holy Script they started out with on the sands of the desert floor at Sinai.

It is the recorded documents and archaeological excavations that measure the sand kingdom. There is no nation in ancient history that has as extensive and complete records of its beginnings and development as Abraham's sand-people of the Middle East. Every day, throughout the world those ancient records are read and put on display in public gatherings in religious liturgies and sermons. They speak of the promises God made to Abraham.

It was there on that desert floor at Sinai, under the clear-night skies, that the nascent form of Israel would look up into the distant stars and view another coming kingdom of future descendants of Abraham: the church, including Jews and Gentile peoples of earth.

THE STAR KINGDOM

In the Old Testament, God was married to Israel. The arrangements for carrying a promised Messianic offspring to term in this union happened at Sinai when He chose to give written laws, instructions of a worship system, and a building wherein He would dwell. These were the instruments of infrastructure needed to build, sustain, and merge a backward tribal people into a unit who would evolve into nationhood. It would take fifteen hundred years of gestation by this sand kingdom to produce the promised seed of the woman who would bruise the head of the serpent.

With prophecies of a coming Messiah, the impregnated nation of Israel would carry her promised unborn child through centuries of great perils and difficulties. There were times when the fetus of Messianic promise came near being aborted by Israel herself with the influence of foreign deities and idol worship. To save Israel and the promised child she carried, God took extreme measures of discipline and confinement through the use of the Assyrians, Babylonians, and others. As she waited for the last days of her delivery, the seat of Roman power unknowingly participated in the fulfillment of prophecy of this birth by issuing a decree that the whole Roman world should be taxed. Mary, the wife-surrogate, on the behalf of the nation of Israel, made her journey to Bethlehem so that in the "fullness of time God could send forth His Son, born of a woman." Though Mary would bear the physical pain of the birth of her son, it was Israel, under the care of Abraham's God, who brought the birth to full-term. Even after His birth, instructions were given to Joseph to flee to Egypt for his protection from those who wished Him dead.

As Egypt was part of the history of Abraham's sand-people being preserved, she would also contribute to Abraham's Star descendant being protected from the wicked Herod. Whereas the sand-people vacated their land of slavery in Egypt in great numbers to begin the formation of nation-building to create a national womb for the birth of the Messiah, Abraham's first star Offspring would also exit Egypt but in the form of one

infant child. The shadows of prophecy about the second exodus from Egypt lay quiet down through the centuries until the act of stepping across the Egyptian border brought fulfillment to Scripture. It can be said that God used common geography to preserve Abraham's sand and promised Star offspring during their stages of infancy:

> Behold, the angel of the Lord appeareth to Joseph in a dream, saying, arise, and take the young child and his mother and flee into Egypt, and be thou there until I bring thee word: for Herod will seek the young child to destroy him. When he arose, he took the young child and his mother by night, and departed into Egypt and was there until the death of Herod: that it might be fulfilled which was spoken of the Lord by the prophet, saying, *out of Egypt have I called my son.* (Matt.2:13-15 KJV)

God's promise to Abraham was that his seed would be as numerous as "the stars of the heaven" and that his seed would "bless the nations." Abraham's descendants would fall into two categories: those of the earth, the sand issue, and those of another world, a spiritual kingdom over which Christ would rule. The New Testament star kingdom is introduced with nighttime scenes. Shepherds were watching over their sheep under the star-lit skies when the announcement of the birth that would bless the nations came to them. It was later when a star guided the wise men of the East to the home of the Promised One. The first arrivals came from the nearby Judean hills at night; the second group came later from afar, with gifts in hand. The wise men were part of a sequential prelude of what would follow in history: "In thee shall all families of the earth be blessed." Jesus spoke of this when He said, "Other sheep I have which are not of this fold: them also I must bring, and they shall hear my voice and there shall be *one fold*, and *one shepherd* (John 10:16 KJV).

There were two distinct groups of people who went to Bethlehem 2000 years ago to worship the Child of the sand-people: the shepherds from the local nearby hills, and the later visitors, the wise men from afar. Each group represented chronological shadows that would be cast over the destinies of the peoples of earth.

The nearby sand people were first to hear the news of the birth of their Offspring. Jesus showed this chronology when He instructed His disciples where and to whom they were to herald the message of His good news: "Do not go among the Gentiles or enter any town of the Samaritans. Go rather to the lost sheep of Israel" (Matt. 10:5 NIV). The sand nation of the house of Israel would be first in line to receive the message of life.

It was our Lord's death and resurrection that gave birth to the star kingdom, and the Great Commission that followed offered membership to both Jew and Gentile. For one to see Abraham's sand issue one must look down on the earth at ethnicity and geography; for a full view of his star descendants, one must look upwards to the heavens.

Jews and Gentiles do not occupy the sand kingdom together as one fold. However, believing Jews and Gentiles are made one people as members in Abraham's Star-Kingdom ruled over by Christ, the head of the church.

My beloved and devoted late wife was Jewish, born of a Jewish mother, and was counted as one of the members of the sand community. Because she accepted Jesus as the Messiah and believed He was the fulfillment of Old Testament prophecy, she had dual membership: one given to her by natural birth being born of a Jewish mother, the other by choice. Her Jewish ancestry had its origins in the sand community with one side of her family having lived in Moscow and fleeing when Napoleon invaded the burning city in 1812. With subsequent pogroms in Russia, they migrated to Romania, then to Ellis Island in the early 1900s. The other side of her family came from Western Europe in the early 1800s, settled in San Francisco and became prosperous professional people. It was before World War II that my wife's mother joined the star-studded membership of the invisible mystical body of Christ upon hearing the message of Yeshua. During her lifetime, her dual citizenship of the sand and star kingdoms afforded her the opportunity of shining her starlight on other grains of sand along the seashore.

It was not the Gentile world that gave us the Bible, it was the Jewish people numbered among the sand community. The doctrines of the New Testament church flowed through the sand people. Everything that the church is and hopes to be now, and in the world to come, has its origins from Jewish voices and writings of the past. Those who postulate the indefensible doctrine of replacement theology, a belief that God has replaced Israel with the church and that He will no longer deal with them as a people with geography, join the ranks of those who practice subtle anti-Semitism and avoid the whole counsel of God. God has not forgotten His promise to Abraham's sand people. Their prolificacy, geography, and restoration are on schedule. The Apostle Paul emphasizes this truth to the Gentile Christians in his letter to the church at Rome.

Today, I remind my Jewish friends and relatives that Christianity wasn't established and spread by the late-coming wise men from afar, the Gentiles, but by the locals of the Judean hills. It was after the church was well established among the Jews, by the Jews, that the late-coming Gentiles entered the fold by the preaching of the gospel by a Hellenized Jew—the Apostle Paul. The world beyond the Judean hills awaited the message of light from the star people: "And they shall declare my glory among the Gentiles" (Isa. 66:19 KJV). It was the sand people who first became the stars of another kingdom of a different dimension that spread the message of the promised Messiah.

Unlike the visible and measurable sand descendants on the seashore that represented physical Israel, the wife of God in the Old Testament, the stars of the heavens were of another order that spoke of a light that would lighten the Gentiles. Prophecy, in the tapestry of Scripture, serves as brilliant pieces of thread interwoven to reveal where we have been in history and where we are going in the future. Pictures of truth carved on the walls of recorded Scripture are immovable, never to be altered, defaced, or lost, now or in the world to come. When entering the inner chambers of these biblical walls, one of the most prominent scenes that stares the visitor in the face is the record of the fulfillment of God's promise to Abraham and his prolific sand and star progeny. Even our Lord reminds us of God's promise to Abraham: "Your father Abraham rejoiced to see my day: and he saw it, and was glad" (John 8:56 KJV).

Chapter 5

Leave and Cleave

Therefore shall a man leave his father and his mother, and shall cleave unto his wife: and they shall be one flesh. (Gen. 2:24 KJV)

The first marriage in the Garden was a microcosmic picture of another marriage to come in the fullness of time. The highest species of God's creation, Adam and Eve, would not only become God-like with His breath of life, which separated them from the animal kingdom, but the species itself would participate under natural law the procreation of the same image-like creation in its offspring. To accomplish this, God established the institution of marriage by joining two opposite genders who would leave their biological parents to form one union. Of all the mysteries in God's creation, the marriage union, the leaving and cleaving, would form the foundation of an ordered society and speak to a transcendent truth.

Successful marriages start with leaving. Voluminous books have been written by professionals offering help and guidance in marriage issues. They concur that the major part of creating a flourishing nuclear family begins with the model of leaving and cleaving. It's marriage 101.

Leaving one's family to form a union in marriage is an adjustment for family members of both parties—the one leaving and those staying at home. Every family knows the empty space left in the absence of a family member after a celebrated marriage, and in our Western society the emptiness comes even before the ceremony: the courting time, the physical absence from the family, and sometimes a certain mental inattention and preoccupation by the party preparing to leave—a prelude to the final event.

Bible truths often come to us over the rails of what is common and familiar. The marriage institution is very common, and when our Lord sets out to find Himself a bride, He applies the principle of leaving His earthly family in this pursuit. Three of the four Gospel writers, Matthew, Mark, and Luke cite the occasion that tells His story of leaving His earthly family. Luke's record reads:

> It was told Him by certain which said, thy mother and thy brethren stand without, desiring to see thee. And He answered and said unto them, my mother and my brethren are these which hear the word of God, and do it. (Luke 8:20-21 KJV)

The words of Jesus might have sounded harsh and uncaring for His family on that day, but the incident showed the principle of leaving His family for a prospective mystical bride. Only the imagination could ponder the feelings inside Jesus' family members when He spoke those words, especially His mother.

Joseph, Jesus' adopted father, was not on the scene at this stage of His life. It must be assumed at this eventful time he was deceased and Mary was cared for by her children. Joseph had followed the tradition of an old Jewish proverb, "To not teach a son a trade was to teach him to steal." Joseph had taught Jesus the trade of carpentry—his own trade. As the oldest son in the family, He would carry the responsibility of being in charge, the custom of that day. We can see the family's dependence on Him when He was present with them at the celebration of a wedding at Cana (John 2:1-8). His mother went to Him for advice and help when the wine was depleted. Her act of dependence on Him came from who He was, and because He was her firstborn.

There were two dramatic stages in Mary's life, and they both began and ended with her firstborn. At a young age, she had been chosen to give birth to God: Deity conceived and formed inside her womb of mortal motherhood. Unlike a modern surrogate, who volunteers a womb for in vitro fertilization for a couple who cannot have children, Mary was conceived by the Holy Spirit. One of her reproductive eggs containing twenty-three chromosomes, the ancestral genetic linkage to the Davidic dynasty, was selected by the Holy Spirit to be used to form the miraculous embryo Who was destined to rule the world. She was the chosen birthmother representing national Israel and would carry that euphoric memory throughout her lifetime.

The role of motherhood fulfillment and the joys of belonging came to a sudden change on that eventful day when Mary went to visit Jesus with her family. During her Son's lifetime, she had carried within her heart hidden memories of her special Son: the angelic announcement of His birth, her labor in Bethlehem, His early childhood, and her natural instincts of motherhood. She had passed on to Him her genes, the DNA of the royal house of David, fully man and all God. That day, for Mary, He was her son—fully man—she had the experience of birth and pain to prove it. However, the epic point every mother experiences when a loving offspring leaves for someone else in marriage had knocked at her heart's door. Her motherly instincts told her she had a competitor; He had chosen another. Forced to see all that was in her heart, motherhood surrendered to what she knew—He was all God. He had left her home on a journey in search of someone else. She remembered when He was lost in Jerusalem at the age of twelve and found Him conversing with the scholars at the temple—today, she had lost Him again, but for a different reason.

The last powerful scene of Jesus leaving His mother for another was described by John, the Apostle, while the two were together at His crucifixion. In the act of giving His life, the ultimate dowry price for His bride, final arrangements of leaving His mother were made:

> When Jesus saw his mother there, and the disciple whom he loved standing nearby, he said to his mother, "Dear woman, here is your son," and to the disciple,

"Here is your mother." From that time on, this disciple took her into his home. (John 19:26, 27 NIV)

One of the most touching scenes in the Bible was just before the curtain closed on the greatest drama of human history. Jesus was suffering on the cross, and He took time to consider the welfare of His devoted and loving mother. As the firstborn of the family, He transferred His earthly responsibility of caring for his mother to John, the one who stood by Him to the end. In doing this, he brought closure and finality to their earthly journey: she was given another son to take His place in this life. This would give us cause to ponder if this were the moment Jesus anticipated when He showed special concern over John, whom He loved.

Prophecy has the extremes of drama when it debuts on the stage of fulfillment. Jesus was His mother's seed, the seed of the woman who would crush the head of Satan. Both were in the throes of fulfilling personal prophecy. While Jesus suffered for his espoused, Mary bore the pain of sorrow. That day, below the cross, the scene of her son suffering in agony brought to mind the words of Simeon thirty-three years earlier: "A sword shall pierce through thine own soul." What was happening before her eyes was not the joyful news coming from the angel, Gabriel, about the birth of a Savior. It was cold foreboding silence, the thrust of stabbing pain, worse than death itself; but Mary, the mother, was also chosen for this hour. Her destiny with Deity inside her body more than three decades earlier had come full circle: she had borne Him in the pain of labor and would bid Him farewell in the sword of sorrow. Without angels, shepherds, and wise men she would watch God push her son through the crucible of another birth canal that would give life to another world and another kingdom— His espoused, the called-out ones. Now her virgin-birthed Son was leaving her permanently for another. Though she suffered the pains of motherhood, claimed Him as her son, she released Him and all those things hidden in her heart to God. Both had finished their earthly journeys together; He was leaving her to cleave to another. The time had come for a new mystery to cover Mary like a cloud—she who had given birth to God would now bid Him farewell in the sword of sorrow and soon join the body of the espoused He was giving His life for.

Simeon said
unto
Mary,..."Yea
a sword shall
pierce
through thine
own soul
also."

Chapter 6

Arranged Marriages in Bible Times

Thomas, because thou hast seen me, thou hast believed: blessed are they that have not seen, and yet have believed. (John 20:29 KJV)

The Bible and the truths that come from it flow through the language of the ancients, and though its truth is universally conceptual, it comes brushed with the colors of the writers' human cultural experience. For one to glean the finer pickings of truth, knowing the culture and customs contemporary with the writers only sharpens the cutting edge that comes from sacred Script. To understand Scripture that embellishes truth about the mystical union of Christ and His espoused, it is helpful to look at the institution of arranged marriages from early history when women were considered chattel, property to be bought and sold in marriage unions. Today, we soften the terms, "bought and sold," by using the word dowry.

Western civilization, as we know it today, is relatively new on the stage of world history when placed on a timeline from the beginning. Whatever one's definition is of the West, it will always include the freedom of personal choice in one's marriage partner.

Other regions of the globe still practice in varied forms the antithesis of this Western custom.

Arranged marriages are what the world has known from almost the beginning of time. It's a natural derivative from the need to create and maintain physical, social, and financial security. Under this system, women and men are paired together, not for the love factor, but rather to serve as glue to maintain established social structures that benefit the families of the two parties to be married. If love results from this arrangement, it occurs after marriage. Unfortunately, this arranged marriage system had a natural evolvement toward consanguinity.

Consanguineous marriages are marriages between close relatives. This is an ancient practice and is as old as history. Abraham, Isaac, and Jacob married close relatives: Abraham married his half-sister, Sarah; Isaac married a cousin, and Jacob, his son, married two first cousins. This system of arranged marriages within a clan is a longstanding tradition in the Middle East, and to this day, a prominent cultural trait even among some groups that have migrated to the West. Historically, it provided posterity for the progenitor and centralized wealth under the control of the family or clan. In less-developed societies, it was used as a survival mechanism. In modern times, especially in Europe and the Middle East, it works against loyalty to a state and fails to engender a spirit of national patriotism. The best illustration of this is found among the Palestinians who are street fighting each other section-by-section in Gaza and other major cities in that area—all by the clans that consanguineous marriages have created. The internal Palestinian conflict between clans loses its front-page coverage because of the ongoing conflict with Israel.

What served historically as a system to preserve and perpetuate a rural community has now become the hammer that creates havoc to its own society in a modern world. Apart from close relative-marriages being an impediment in fostering statehood, its practice potentiates grave health issues such as lower IQs and genetic disorders.

During the period when the church moved westward into Europe, it saw consanguineous marriages as a threat to unity and harmony in a Christian society. To alter this, the church imposed a prohibition against relative marriages down to the fourth cousin. This required a clan or tribe to go outside its group for marriage arrangements; hence, the prohibition broke down inimical conflicts between clan groups, thus promoting greater cohesion with common goals and interest. These rules imposed by the church helped Europe evolve into major states instead of fragmented clans. However, though we value results of the church's decisions in changing marriage rules, we are left with the biblical custom of arranged marriages to understand the deeper meaning of Christ and His church.

There is an old Jewish saying spoken by men, "I thank God for two things: that I'm not a Gentile and wasn't born a woman." This speaks to the subordinate role of women in ancient biblical society where women had little legal standing, and in many cases were considered chattel.

The arranged marriage scene during Bible times showed the subordinate role of the woman when she was considered for marriage: she was property to be sold by one family and bought by another. The usual practice was to draw up a legal contract within the circle of the clan group or family. In biblical times, marriage was not an agreement between two people, but between two families. The general custom was that the fathers of the two families entered into a contract agreement where payment was made to the girl's family in the form of a dowry. When the servant of Abraham went to Haran to seek a bride for Isaac, the payment of silver, gold, and raiment were made to family members. Sometimes the dowry was not given in the form of gold or silver, but in service. In Genesis, Jacob made this arrangement with Laban, his uncle, for payment of Rachel and Leah, his first cousins.

The arranged marriage always came with two separate ceremonies with celebrations at both events. The first celebration came after the two families completed the formal agreement, at which time the dowry payment was made where agreements were reached and sworn to like any chattel property purchase. This was called the betrothal, and the woman became legally married to the father's son though she would remain at her home until the second event. The latter part of the arranged marriage would finalize the union when the purchaser took possession of his property. The son would go to the home of the bride at a later date with his entourage and take his espoused to his father's home where a great celebration was planned. Some considered the betrothal the more significant of the two events.

The circumstances surrounding the birth of Jesus show in great detail the culture of arranged marriages. God waits until Mary is espoused to Joseph before Gabriel announces that she is chosen to give birth to the Messiah. Mary was considered married to Joseph when the announcement came. The first stage of marriage had been finalized, the families had met, agreements were reached with celebrations, and both waited for the final wedding celebration. However, Joseph found her to be pregnant, which was grounds for divorce, and being a "just man," he took measures to litigate it privately until the intervention of the Lord through a dream. Though Mary's pregnancy occurred before the final stage of the marriage arrangement, there was no community disgrace as long as Joseph took her to his home. "Then Joseph being raised from sleep did as the angel of the Lord had bidden him, and took unto him his wife…and knew her not till she had brought forth her firstborn son" (Matt. 1:24,25 KJV).

The New Testament writers had a strong grasp on the truth that the church was Christ's bride in waiting, the chosen one for the Son of the Father, and that the dowry price and legal arrangements had been made at Calvary.

If we juxtaposed the arranged marriage custom of Bible times with the collective body of teaching from Jesus and the Apostles about the church, we would find distinct parallel truths of the heavenly order. However,the heavenly pattern changes the premise of marriage from the earthly. Whereas the earthly marriage arrangement was based on legal purchase without consideration of a prerequisite of love, the mystery marriage from heaven begins the marriage contract signing only because of a predisposition of love for the espoused; and for the expression of that love, the Son himself attends the contract signing by offering his body as the purchase price for His Beloved.

There is further expansion of this truth when Peter uses the arranged marriage custom by turning it on end. With arranged marriages, couples in many cases never meet until the wedding. There is no dating or courting as in Western society; if love happens, it occurs after marriage. This is an abhorrent thought for us in the West—imagine meeting your wedding partner for the first time on the day you're to be married and living with that person the rest of your life. Peter shows the new love-faith arrangement the church has in her engagement to Christ by introducing the culture of a higher law—the law of love, which is in contrast with the arranged marriage: "Though you have not seen him, you love him; and even though you do not see him now, you believe in him and are filled with an inexpressible and glorious joy" (1 Peter 1:8 NIV). Peter points out that Jesus changes the natural order of arranged marriages where neither party loves each other between the dowry gift (the legal contract signing) and the wedding event. Christ's betrothal to His future wife included something more than just the dowry gift of His life: it was the promise that He would send another person in His place to translate

His feelings to the espoused until He came to take her to His Father's home. Though the bride-to-be, the church, will never see the one who paid the dowry price until the wedding day, she learns to know and love Him by faith from the whispers of the Holy Spirit, the one sent to represent Him. Through those soft quiet whispers, she learns to love Him and prepares herself for His arrival to take her to the wedding event.

Jesus spoke of this period between betrothal and marriage when He said to Thomas after He arose from the dead, "Blessed are they that have not seen, and yet have believed" (John 20:29 KJV).

Even in the Roman world, the early church understood the culture of arranged marriages. Though urbanized Roman cities were less dependent on traditional marriage arrangements, it was still practiced, and was no doubt prevalent in the church at Rome. When Paul wrote to the church in Rome, the believers who lived in the culture of arranged marriages understood the deeper meaning of Romans 8:29: "For those God foreknew He also predestined to be conformed to the likeness of his Son..." (Rom. 8:29 NIV). The truth of this verse can stealthily slip by us if we don't understand arranged marriages of that day. The Roman believer, whether Jewish or Gentile, understood it well.

It was the father of the groom who selected and gave approval of the espoused; hence, the father would have known the prospective bride prior to the engagement contract. The young girl was an investment who would be vetted before approval. If approved, she was destined to become part of his family through a legal marriage contract.

In the Scriptures, predestination is associated with foreknowledge. "Those, whom He foreknew, He predestined…" Paul shows the omniscience of God's order and purpose in the life of the believer, who through foreknowledge, will be chosen. Moreover, unlike the traditional marriage arrangement where the girl has no voice in choosing her life's partner, God's selection of the girl for His Son in marriage is based solely on her freedom of choice—her free will.

There is no greater love found than in the marriage union. It was designed to be so in the creation of man and woman so as to picture the higher order of love between Christ and the church. Paul said, "Now we see but a poor reflection in a mirror; then we shall see face to face" (1 Cor. 13:12 NIV). The marriage picture of love may be the purest form of truth for us down here on earth to understand Christ's love for the church, but it pales in comparison to the reality of what awaits the church in the world to come.

Chapter 7

The Two Women Riders of Genesis and Revelation

Thou shalt go unto my country, and to my kindred, and take a wife unto my son Isaac...And the servant took ten camels of the camels of his master, and departed...and the servant brought forth jewels of silver, and jewels of gold, and rainment, and gave them to Rebekah...And Rebekah arose, and her damsels, and they rode upon the camels, and followed the man...And Isaac took Rebekah and she became his wife; and he loved her. (Gen. 24:4, 10, 53, 61, 67 KJV)

I saw a woman sit upon a scarlet coloured beast, full of names of blasphemy, having seven heads and ten horns...And the woman was arrayed in purple and scarlet colour, and decked with gold and precious stones and pearls...the ten horns which thou sawest upon the beast, these shall hate the whore, and shall make her desolate and naked. (Rev. 17:3, 4, 16 KJV)

The Bible shows two women riders who use two different types of beasts to achieve two distinct objectives. The first woman is seen riding on a camel in the book of Genesis; the other woman makes her debut in

Revelation, the last book, riding upon a metamorphosed creature of power and authority. The camel rider in Genesis is a poor peasant girl dressed in a drab common manner who knows that her role and wealth status will change the moment she reaches the end of her journey. The rider on the beast in Revelation is robed in attire worn only among the rich and powerful and is at the pinnacle of her success. Both women have antithetical roles and dramatic closures in their lives. The rider on the beast, dressed in royal clothing, who has proudly and arrogantly allowed herself to be compromised by the sovereigns of earth, succumbs to poverty and rejection by her state-clients; whereas the lady on the camel rides with commanding virtue, with a fairy-tale ending by getting position, wealth, and the prince in the end. Both carry the type-images of the Christian church: the camel rider, the chosen true church, whose interest is in fulfilling her commitment to the one who has paid her dowry, whom having not seen, she loves; the other rider, an imposter apostate church, whose objectives are to gain power and acceptance through violence and moral compromise.

In close examination of the two women riders, the story of the peasant camel-rider in Genesis becomes meaningful by looking forward to her future in the coming church age. The affluent metaphorical beast-rider in Revelation is understood by looking backward into her past.

THE WOMAN WHO RODE THE CAMEL

One of the greatest human-interest stories in the Old Testament is found in the record of a wealthy nobleman who sends his loyal servant to Haran, a region in modern-day Turkey, to secure a bride for his son, Isaac. It is an account without violence, greed, or fear. To understand the intrigue of this event, one must understand the cultural context of arranged marriages of that day. If one picture is worth a thousand words, then looking at a series of them from this story will make most of us take a vow of silence. The Bible is full of well-painted pictures about events that reach beyond the story itself. One of the greatest is found on the canvas of Genesis 24, a love story about a young bride on top of a camel riding with a caravan across the rugged terrain of the ancient, well-traveled Fertile Crescent. Her guardian and protector, who arranges the legal transfer of the dowry under her father's roof, is prepared to take all measures necessary to see that she is delivered safely.

Little is known about Eliezer, Abraham's servant, the one assigned to make the crossing into northern Mesopotamia to buy a bride for Isaac. We know he was from Damascus and the steward in charge of everything Abraham possessed. Abraham was like a nomadic king, living in tents ruling over a large number of people whose direct loyalty was to him, either in the legal form of slavery of that day or indentured servitude. In one incident, Abraham took more than 300 trained men, born in his own house, to confront a marauding band to retrieve his nephew who had been taken captive. In ancient times, close household loyalty and dependence upon a person of power and position were the first cousins to the institution of slavery. In those early days, common interest and group survival lived alongside slavery.

Eliezer had proven himself a loyal and faithful manager over Abraham's empire and was equipped by experience and leadership to be given the task of bringing back safely a bride for his son. His leadership became obvious upon his arrival in Haran. Instead of following the traditional protocol of greeting the leader of Abraham's clan in Haran first, he proceeded to the place where only women would be found: the city water well. According to custom, only women carried water.

Feminine beauty has always been admired by the male gender and is recorded as such in this narrative. However, Eliezer attempts to look beyond the natural beauty of any girl coming to draw water at this city well. In his prayer, he asks God:

> Let it come to pass, that the damsel to whom I shall say, let down thy pitcher, I pray thee, that I may drink; and she shall say, drink, and I will give thy camels drink also: let the same be she that thou hast appointed for thy servant Isaac. (Genesis 24:14 KJV)

Eliezer was not only a loyal subject to his master, he was dedicated to Abraham's God. It was the reach beyond the customary drink for a stranger that the servant was wanting—the second mile, a voluntary act of watering the camels that would reveal a certain depth of character and energy beyond the girl's natural beauty. Eliezer was a leader among men; he knew what traits to look for when selecting people for specific responsibilities and roles:

> And when she had done giving him drink, she said, I will draw water for thy camels also, until they have done drinking. (Genesis 24:19 KJV)

The servant of Abraham had taken ten camels on his trip to Haran. Camels have a large capacity for water, and a single dromedary can drink up to 30 gallons at one watering. Rebekah had committed herself to a tremendous task of drawing water for ten camels. The servant's ten camels required as much as 300 gallons of water at a total weight of approximately 2400 pounds. This was an enormous chore for a young lady, and in all likelihood, she had other women from her village to assist. Because it was customary for men not to draw water at the community well, Rebekah was left alone to do all the work. The servant and the men with him watched as she labored. Young Rebekah was not aware that the hard work of drawing water from the well for thirsty camels would give her a new life in another country with great wealth.

This well was the first one recorded in Scripture that would serve as a meeting-place where a woman's life would be changed forever because of a stranger asking for a drink of water. The second record would be at Jacob's well in Samaria eighteen hundred years later, when another woman would be asked for a drink from a stranger. This first scene of a man asking for a drink of water from a woman was well rehearsed and painted on the canvas of time for the one that would follow in another age. History has a way of repeating itself, and this hidden truth glistens for us today with two wells, two women, and two strangers asking for a drink of water.

After the young lady's act of service in watering the ten camels, the servant then made his response to Rebekah by giving her a gold ring and two golden bracelets. At this point, Rebekah knew something big was happening. The outright gift of the wealth of gold was too large a payment from a stranger for simply drawing water for his camels. Rebekah had been chosen.

The next best thing in a family in Rebekah's day, besides having a son, was to have a daughter who could bring a good dowry; Rebekah was this and much more. The chosen chaste damsel and family consented to the arranged marriage, the dowry was paid, and the next morning she said goodbye to her family, friends, and her known world. With ten camels, the caravan departed under the supervision of the servant whose mission now was to deliver a bride to his master in another land and a new people.

Today, one's estate is passed on to the next generation either by a will, a living trust, or by the court of law (if one dies intestate). In ancient times, to ensure posterity and defense against the erosion of concentrated wealth, family strength, and position, the property in an estate was passed on to the eldest son. To do otherwise would break apart the family's collective power and influence. Generally, the surviving siblings became dependent upon the oldest brother and came under his authoritarian rule. Abraham was at the center of this cultural tradition that was practiced in ancient Mesopotamia, his former homeland. This practice was later altered in Moses' day to include others in the nuclear family. However, Abraham would reverse the tradition; he had a younger son, Isaac, who had been chosen to be his sole heir. Genesis 24 gives a clear description of the culture and traditions in Abraham's day when a notable figure of power and wealth arranges a marriage for his son. To ensure that his dynasty and position will be maintained with his son after his demise, he chooses to bring a wife for Isaac from his own family living in Haran, a place more than 400 miles away. There are reasons for Abraham taking this action: the continued consolidation of his wealth within his own ethnicity, and loyalty to the voice of God, "In Isaac shall thy seed be called" (Gen. 21:12 KJV). In ancient times, the passing on of wealth and position to a descendant had a greater guarantee if marriages were arranged within one's own tribal and family group. In Abraham's case, to avoid assimilation into the local community, he needed to secure a bride for his sole heir from outside the community he lived in. Abraham wanted his son to marry a close relative, a pervasive practice in the Middle East even today.

In the natural order of events of Abraham bringing a bride for his son from a faraway place, the Scriptures present an awe-inspiring scene of a picture-within-a-picture of what is to come in the future when God will purchase a bride for His Son from another land. The narrative of the story shows the calm, persuasive execution of the servant's responsibilities in transferring the dowry payment of gold and gifts. Because of the servant's peaceful and kind nature, Rebekah believes and trusts the voice of the gentle person on a special mission. For the first time in her life, she is singled out and becomes the center of attention. When the customary legal transactions are completed, she begins her journey to another country on a reliable and robust beast of burden—a camel.

From ancient times down to modern history, camels were the miracle beasts for carrying loads with great endurance. They were the symbols of wealth and known to be ships of the desert. A camel could go 5 to 7 days with little food or water and lose a quarter of its body weight. They had long thin legs with powerful muscles that carried heavy loads over great distances. A strong camel was able to carry as much as 900 pounds, but the usual and more comfortable load was in the range of 330. The walking speed was 3 miles per hour, and a caravan would normally travel 25 miles a day. A fully-grown camel could weigh up to 1500 pounds. Not only were they a beast of burden, the female camel provided milk, up to 4 liters daily, which had greater nourishment value than that of a cow or goat, and its vitamin C gave special help to people making long distant treks. It was upon and among these animals that Rebekah would make her passage to a new land.

Rebekah's journey from her family's region to her chosen new land was wrought with many dangers and perils. With the ten camels carrying the necessary supplies and equipment for overland travel and nightly camping, predators and thieves lurked about on the lonely narrow paths under the settled stillness of the night. There was always greater safety in numbers. The men sent along with Eliezer, Abraham's servant, were well-trained warriors. Caravans in those days traveled over the safest routes and camped at night in secured areas. The journey probably took them between two and four weeks.

Upon the caravan's arrival, Rebekah sees Isaac walking from the well, Lahai-roi, which means in literal translation, "Well of the Living One, my Beholder." Even the well from which Isaac comes to greet Rebekah embellishes the romantic adventure of the story. The saga of Rebekah begins and ends with two water wells: the first being in the village where she is chosen, the second, the place where she meets Isaac going out to greet her:

> And Isaac came from the way of the well Lahai-roi...and behold, the camels were coming....And Isaac took Rebekah, and she became his wife; and he loved her. (Gen. 24:62, 63, 67 KJV)

There is no greater story describing the planning and efforts put forth by one party to secure a bride for a son.

Rebekah had chosen to leave her family, suffer the arduous trip aboard the camel, and deliver herself to her espoused as a chaste virgin. Her status was changed legally when the dowry payment was made in her father's tent in Haran, and upon arrival at her new dwelling Isaac gives permanence to that legal contract.

There is concealed treasure in this old account of the lady camel rider. What one sees beyond the record itself rises above the story. Rebekah is the true church in allegorical form. She is the chosen chaste bride, birthed on the day of Pentecost and given a Guide to make the trip across the rugged terrain of history, choosing to be faithful despite the hardships in front of her. Today, still atop the camel, with the Holy Spirit as her guide, she moves on in her journey to meet the Nobleman's Son who will appear as the "Well of the Living One," and "Unto them that look for Him shall He appear" (Heb. 9:28 KJV). The gentle quiet voice of the servant leading the caravan still directs the way, and the rider on the camel only becomes more determined and focused as she nears her new permanent home.

THE MYSTERY WOMAN RIDER ON THE MUTATED BEAST

The ancient Greeks and Romans were always giving a human face to everything. The prophetic picture of the final state of the church follows this literary and metaphorical tradition in Holy Script by depicting the moral and spiritual condition of the church with the human face of a woman:

> I saw a woman sit upon a scarlet-colored beast, full of names of blasphemy, having seven heads and ten horns. And upon her forehead was a name written, MYSTERY BABYLON THE GREAT, THE MOTHER OF HARLOTS AND ABOMINATIONS OF THE EARTH. And I saw the woman drunk with the blood of the saints, and with the blood of the martyrs of Jesus. (Rev.17:3, 5, 6 KJV)

Not all treasures in the Bible evoke elation; some bear the message of pain for what has happened, or what waits in the future. In Rome today, one is made to remember some of the pain Jesus spoke about when he wept over Jerusalem. In 70 A.D., Jerusalem fell to the Romans; the Temple was sacked and destroyed and the spoils of war taken off to Rome. Today, tourists visit the Roman Forum to view the Arch of Titus that depicts the famous relief showing the contents taken from the Jewish Temple, the centerpiece being the huge seven-branched menorah being carried in triumph down Rome's Via Sacra. The Arch was designed and built after Titus's death in 81 A.D. to honor him and his victory over the Jews. Though today it is an attraction for art and culture, tears fall from the hearts of those who visit the site who know the sacked Temple's history. To this day, many Jews refuse to walk underneath the monumental arch. This event in history marked the beginning of the Jewish Diaspora throughout Europe. Jesus predicted the Temple destruction to His disciples: "There shall not be left here one stone upon another that shall not be thrown down" (Mark 13:2 KJV).

The woman riding upon the beast in the book of Revelation falls into this category, a picture of unpleasant things of the past, veiled with a prophecy of doom. Unlike the first lady on the camel who makes her journey in simplicity, this woman is on a powerful beast and has used it to aggrandize for herself wealth and power. At this stage of her inordinate dalliances, the rider and beast have a symbiotic relationship: both need each other to achieve what each wants. The mystery woman represents everything the camel rider is not: she seeks temporal power and wealth and uses liaisons with kings to achieve her objective; the camel rider keeps herself pure for the person she will marry when her journey is completed.

Mystery Babylon's equestrian roots, though the beast she rides is not that of a horse, take her back to her religious primitive infancy during Nebuchadnezzar's Babylonian Empire. Her future will carry her all the way to Europe's ten toes on Daniel's image (Dan. 2:40-43), the fourth and final kingdom of the Gentile age. She is presented as an anthropomorphic symbol of that part of the visible religious system that has hijacked the Christian religion and embodies the symbol of politicized religion that comes to power because of her influence upon the masses. In this position of special honor and privilege, she provides services to the state at the expense of the church. This rider is a mystery woman, a composite picture of how religious systems are used by the state to promote the state's welfare. We have come to understand the allegorical meaning of the story of the woman upon the camel by looking forward to the church age. To understand Mystery Babylon in Revelation and her religious institutional link that gives meaning to her symbolic image requires looking backward in time:

> Nebuchadnezzar, the king made an image of gold, whose height was threescore cubits, and the breadth of it six cubits; he set it up in the plain of Dura, in the province of Babylon. When all the people heard the sound of the music, all the people, the nations, and the languages fell down, and worshiped the golden image that Nebuchadnezzar the king, had set up. (Daniel 3:1,7 KJV)

Religion and state have always been interdependent Siamese twins from early man. One needs only to read the history of ancient Egypt to understand this compelling force that forged century-after-century quasi-pagan theocracies. What we have in Daniel with Nebuchadnezzar's image is a window picture, a slice of time, showing this institution in play. The king of Babylon, Nebuchadnezzar, had expanded his empire and imported thousands of conquered peoples into his capital city from subdued areas. Judah was one of these territories. Among these newly forced immigrants from the city of Jerusalem, which was eventually destroyed along with Solomon's Temple, was a young devout Jew of high learning. His name was Daniel, and he was destined to become the great predictor of four coming empires in his part of the world. The Babylonian Kingdom over which Nebuchadnezzar ruled was the first.

Some might say that King Nebuchadnezzar had some degree of administrative genius along with his madness. Nebuchadnezzar knew the power religion had on the masses, that it could serve to unify or be divisive. It was his intent to create a monolithic empire accompanied by a state-sponsored deity that everyone was required to honor and worship.

Religion, in varied forms, has always been a force willing to act in concert with the state to achieve her objectives. The state, on the other hand, makes frequent use of established religious systems to enhance the government's political end. King Nebuchadnezzar followed this custom of using religion to augment civil rule by introducing into a polytheistic world a gigantic deity in a large valley where every member of his vast governmental bureaucracy could congregate and swear allegiance to the king, his government, and his god. His intent was to make all deities subordinate to the one he had made of gold. Loyalty to him and his government was to be measured by his subjects falling down and worshipping his god. Perhaps his newly constructed image was of himself, an attempt at creating a monarchal deification cult, a system used by the later Roman emperors to enhance their political loyalty among the populace by institutionalizing imperial worship.

Nebuchadnezzar had already arranged a painful death for ay who would resist his forced religious exercise: a furnace of fire. Spotters were placed throughout the large mass meeting to observe any non-conforming attendee. Three men of the Jewish Diaspora that had been taken to Babylon were detected being non-compliant with the king's law requiring the worship of the golden image. By refusing to bow, the three Jews had become enemies of the state and were condemned to execution by being thrown into the furnace. What the king attempted to accomplish in a public execution of the resistors was overshadowed by the miracle that happened inside the furnace: the three Jews survived the fire and lived to tell about it.

What the narrative in the book of Daniel allows us to see in Nebuchadnezzar's coerced religious exercise is that despotic governments will use whatever methods are available to them to augment their position of power. Nebuchadnezzar was using state-imposed religious conformity to serve his best interest as head of state. Controlling and subjugating newly acquired deities from his expanded empire was important to his royal posterity. The king intended to compel all deities, including those from newly acquired territories, to be subject to his chosen supreme one that represented the state. His action was an outlined preview of what was to come at the end of days. Future empires that would follow Nebuchadnezzar's would also continue the practice of employing religion as a governing tool to bring together diversity under a centralized state religion.

The temples of ancient Babylon were filled with prostitutes who became part of their religious worship.

This condition of harmonious co-dependency between polytheistic pagan religion and state would continue to exist for centuries until the rise and expansion of a new minority monotheistic group, known as Christians. Under the Roman Empire, this new religious minority refused to participate under that umbrella and was perceived as a threat to the state because they swore allegiance only to one God. The rise of the Christian movement in and around the Mediterranean Sea, and beyond, spread as a grassroots movement. Being a monotheistic minority and refusing to submit as "one among the many," she suffered persecution and rejection by civil authorities but continued to alter the landscape of Europe by increasing her ranks with the conversion of the masses. With polytheism slowly losing its numbers, it lost its grip as the dominant religious influence on society. As Christianity continued to grow in numbers and influence within the Roman Empire, the government of Rome would make a political decision to exchange the historical religious counterpart to the state, the woman of polytheism, in favor of the new dynamic force of Christian monotheism that the masses had accepted. Christianity became the official state religion of the Roman Empire on February 27, 380, through an edict issued by Emperor Theodosius. In 391, the Emperor ruled all cults, except Christianity, prohibited. The Roman Empire had acquired a new official religious counterpart. However, underneath the new face of the ensconced church at the seat of power in Rome, the new was the old

and the old was the new, fully in place as it had always

been, the state using religion for control and governanceof the masses. She would now become the religious institution to Imperial Rome that pagan polytheism was to ancient Babylon.

Rome did not know that when she made Christianity the state religion that the church would evolve into a position of such prominence that she would eventually sit as a queen and hold the reins of power and wealth. The system of state and polytheistic religious co-dependency that was part of ancient Babylon would now become the same institution that would ride the beast in Revelation; the difference would be the change in name and position. Whereas in ancient Babylon, religion was used by the state as less than an equal and was pagan, in Revelation she would be seen as a rider on top of the beast and viewed by many as apostate Christianity. Instead of employing live prostitutes in temple worship, she would prostitute herself with the world system. To some, she is a picture of how a state-sponsored religious system has evolved from the time of Nebuchadnezzar in Babylon, the first of four kingdoms that will arise in the earth, to the time in church history when religion will influence the state as a single rider.

Before Rome declared Christianity the state religion, the Christian movement accreted from the ground upward. It was upon the blood of martyrs in the soil of the earth that they spread the faith; now, imperial Rome offered state protection and promotion. This was the turning point in Western Civilization.

The Christian church that had grown under the

oppressive feet of governments would now ascend to the throne of power inside palaces of gold. The teachings of the church would not come from catacombs and cloistered secret hovels but from the iron hand of decrees with authority and enforcement coming from the armies of the state. She, with her masses, would be destined to become the greatest influence ever in shaping Europe's destiny for good and bad. The mystery woman from Babylon would no longer be subordinate to the state, but mount the beast with legs of iron to crush and destroy the rider's enemies around the Empire. Civil governments would brutally enforce her decrees and act upon her ambitions. The power she possessed would cause sovereigns to tremble at her commands and bow before her feet. The axiom, "Power corrupts, and absolute power tends to corrupt absolutely," would be written throughout much of her history while she rides the beast. She would treat others as she was treated before she mounted the beast. In her original humble beginnings of innocence, she was given life by someone of Semitic origin, yet she would become anti-Semitic, forcing Jews, by the use of the sword, to renounce their Jewish faith. Darkness in Europe was never as deep as when state-sponsored Christendom used the sword to spread state religion on the back of civil authority. Not only did the rider on the beast force conversions by the edge of the sword, the sword was used to destroy her own from within. Reform within the church was rarely an option. John Huss's blood still cries from the earth after he was burned at the
stake for possessing non-Latin Bibles.

Mystery Babylon also held the reins of Protestant state churches. The little-known odious record of some of the Protestant state churches bears the ugly scars of violence against their own who differed doctrinally or who rejected the state church. Many devout Anabaptists suffered death in cruel, barbaric ways at the hands of those who broke from Rome. Unable to separate church from state, Protestantism continued to use the beast of state to exercise its religious control. John Bunyan, author of Pilgrim Progress, spent 12 years in prison for preaching without a license. Catholic state churches were exchanged for state Protestantism; religious liberty and freedom from state control awaited the new world.

Mystery Babylon is not sectarian, but is the composite picture of a religious system that uses the state church for bureaucratic gain, and more specifically, she is the growing tares in the fields of Christendom, the five virgins without oil, and the rich arrogant church of Laodicea.

Revelation describes the woman being intoxicated with the blood of the martyrs: "And I saw the woman drunk with the blood of the saints, and with the blood of the martyrs of Jesus" (Rev. 17:6 KJV).

The image of the Mystery Woman tells the message of her long history after mounting the beast: the record of power, abuse, and violence. John's prophecy shows her indictment and the forthcoming judgment after having compromised herself in the name of religion. Secular empires and dynasties have come and gone and she has outlasted them all. However, recent events of history are telling another story.

THE RIDER'S FALL FROM THE BEAST

> The ten horns which thou sawest upon the beast, these shall hate the harlot, and shall make her desolate and naked and eat her flesh, and burn her with fire…and he cried mightily with a strong voice, saying, Babylon the great is fallen, is fallen, and is become the habitation of demons…for all nations have drunk of the wine of the wrath of her fornication, and the kings of the earth have committed fornication with her, and the merchants of the earth are grown rich through the abundance of her delicacies. (Rev. 17:16; 18:2, 3 KJV)

Something is happening in Europe today that speaks to the fall of the woman from the beast that has carried her through the centuries. The kings who have patronized her in the past are reversing history. When the dissolution of this relationship is complete, it will bring her to abject poverty and ruin. The state at that point will no longer respond to the spell of its mistress. The apostatized bureaucratic power of religion, as European Western Civilization has known it, will fall from the beast and be deemed an enemy of the state. When it is finalized, she will no longer serve as a useful tool for European governments.

The power and influence the woman rider had on the ten-horned beast had been derived from her authority over her adherents in Europe. Her future waits until the time when her religious prostitution will fail to gain favor from the beast she rides upon because the masses will forsake her, leaving her powerless. At that time, she will be viewed as a political liability. The beast will utterly destroy her infrastructure and forbid her existence. History is something one can measure. For centuries, the governments of Europe have been under the influence of a religious system with the face of a decadent woman who is destined to become broken, never to be repaired or restored. The revision of an eighteenth century nursery rhyme succinctly tells her story:

Humpty Dumpty sat on the beast
Humpty Dumpty had a great fall
All the king's horses and all the king's men
Didn't want to put Humpty Dumpty back
together again.

The scene of the fall of the woman from the beast is also George Orwell's *Animal Farm* at its best. The beast of Europe has created a coup-d'etat and taken over the farm, driving into oblivion the farmer who holds the reins of power. Orwell's satirical novel on the rise of communism was written in metaphorical form after the fact; the mystery woman from Babylon was presented also in metaphorical imagery, but in her case, the world waits for it to become fact.

Two crowds are forcing their way into Europe's religious palace courtyard threatening the life of European Christianity: secularists and Islamic immigrants. Both are changing the demographic and political landscapes that tell of disaster and death for the Mystery Woman.

CHRISTIANITY'S DECLINE IN EUROPE

The handwriting that spells decline of the Mystery Woman in Europe is on the wall for the world to see. The traditional religious authority and influence that have emanated from Europe is in decay, and the citadel of the Christian religion, Europe, is under attack by forces unknown in modern times. The opposition to her centuries-old control has crossed the castle moat and is battering her iron gate, the sounds of which are reverberating throughout Christendom.

Governments of Europe are reflecting in their policies the results of the spiritual and moral decline that have permeated their culture. The European Union constitution reflects this new drifting away from the traditional moorings of State churches and religious ties. Even after religious leaders across Europe met with EU leaders for interfaith talks, German Chancellor Angela Merkel went on to say, "The new draft of the European Union constitution will not mention God or Christianity. There is little support among European governments to renegotiate."

The late Pope John Paul II, a voice of conservatism, expressed concern about how Europe was throwing off her religious past and rejecting traditional values when he said, "Europe needed to be re-evangelized." The tide of rejection of Christianity in exchange for a new culture and atmosphere of secularization and relativism is a pronounced gauge that measures where the traditional church is heading. It is losing its influence on massive numbers of adherents who are falling prey to what the New Testament refers to as "the falling away" (II Thess. 2:3).

Throughout Europe, there is a decline in participation in church life and practices. The Catholic church of 1.1 billion members is experiencing growth in Latin America and Africa, but throughout the church's traditional base in Europe a crisis is brewing over loss of membership and interest. Affluence and secularization are pushing aside and rejecting its religious cultural past. Inside some of Europe's largest dioceses in Germany, France, Italy, and Ireland the number of Catholics who attend Mass regularly has slipped as low as 20 percent, and in France fewer than 10 percent of the Catholics attend church regularly. The most Catholic state of all Europe, Ireland, has always been ahead of other European nations in church attendance. In the 1970s, it registered 90 percent in weekly attendance. A recent survey shows the number to be 44 percent. In his book titled *Values in Times of Upheaval,* Pope Benedict XVI suggested that, "In order to survive, Europe needs a critical acceptance of its Christian culture."

In Europe, Christianity is not only declining among Catholics but is also experiencing fading numbers among non-Catholic groups. The estimated church attendance for the Lutheran Church in Sweden, formerly the state religion, is around 1.5 percent. This is also the trend in England. In the 2001 census, 72 percent of Britain listed themselves as Christians, but only about 6.3 percent attended church on any Sunday, a drop from 7.5 percent that was registered in 1998. The chill of religious fervor in the Church of England among its clergy is evidenced by a survey conducted at the University of Wales. It showed that only 60 percent of its clergy believed in the virgin birth of Jesus, and 1 out of 33 Anglican priests doubts the existence of God.

It is significant that while Europe's churchgoing numbers dwindle, in other parts of the world Christianity is expanding rapidly. This is especially striking in view that Europe is the home of many Christian movements. Perhaps it all points to Europe replacing religion with secularism, reason, science, and the power of the individual.

The church is no longer an influence on the state as in the past. Not only is she losing her historical position of authority over the state, she is experiencing competition from Islam with the influx of massive immigration from Islamic countries.

ISLAMIC INVASION OF EUROPE

After World War II, Europe opened the door to foreign workers through a guest-worker program backed by willing politicians and compliant judges. The workers were supposed to stay temporarily, but were given the opportunity for family reunification programs, and the system became a permanent part of the economic expansion of Europe. Many of the subsequent massive waves of immigration into Europe came from Islamic countries, and today, Muslims represent the majority of immigrants in Western European countries, including Belgium, France, Germany, and the Netherlands. They are also the largest group of the immigrant population in the United Kingdom. The exact number of Muslims in Europe is hard to come by because Western censuses rarely ask respondents about their faith. But it is estimated that there may be as many as 23 million Muslims who now call traditional Christian Europe their home and make up to 5 percent of its total population. France has the highest number at about 10 percent. Though Muslims consist of only 3 percent of the British population, those who have researched the statistics project that in thirty-five years there will be twice the number of Muslims in mosques on Friday nights as in Christian churches on Sunday mornings.

Today, the Muslim birth rate in Europe is three times higher than that of the non-Muslim. If current trends continue, the Muslim population of Europe will nearly double by 2015, while the non-Muslim population will shrink by 3.5 percent. Apart from the increase of births among Muslims, upward of 900,000 legal immigrants enter Europe each year, of which most are Muslim. The number of illegal Muslim immigrants entering into Europe is estimated to be 500,000 per year. A typical woman in the Islamic world bears more than 4 children on the average. Many Muslim immigrants who arrive in

Europe have with them their extended families that may include two, three, or four wives plus all their children. Families like these can number as high as 15 people, and in France alone, this means that up to 500,000 people may be living in polygamous families. There are hundreds of polygamous families in Britain, Germany, the Netherlands, and other countries.

At the present population growth trends, combined with the legal and illegal immigration, some believe that in 25 years Europe could have a Muslim majority. It will be at that point, when the traditional European population will have become a minority, that they will remember Winston Churchill's famous quote: "Democracy is the worst form of government except for all those others that have been tried." When Islam dominates the ballot box, democracy will have joined all those others that have been tried.

The Muslims are to Europe in the twenty-first century what the invading Germanic tribes were to the Roman Empire in the fifth century, when they conquered an empire and became Christianized. The difference between the two invasions is that the Islamic campaign today is being done through immigration, population explosion, and eventual dominance at the democratic ballot box. Unlike the Germanic peoples who invaded the Roman World, the Muslims will not be Christianized, but will force their Islamic religion on indigenous populations throughout Europe. Democracy, the icon of the West that has served to give freedom to the developed world, will be the very door which Islam will walk through and change Europe. Christian Europe, the motherland of Christian expansion for hundreds of years, is entering a phase of senescent finality by sliding downward into the caldron of political death.

With the loss of church adherents in Europe and the prospect of a Muslim majority in a few years, the woman rider atop the beast is slipping from her seat of power, and God will call to remembrance her historical legacy of apostasy.

While the Mystery woman from Babylon appears weakened and slipping from her position as the rider on top of the beast of Europe, other parts of the world are rising to proclaim the message of Christ's love, hope, and return. From our point in history, we see the espoused peasant rider with the caravan of ten camels in Genesis marching on, and with her silhouette off in the distance under the evening sunset, excitement looms as she nears the end of her passage for her marriage to the Nobleman's Son.

"And Isaac went out to meditate in the field at eventide: and he lifted up his eyes, and saw, and behold, the camels were coming…and he took Rebekah, and she became his wife."

Chapter 8

The Bible's Three Marriages

THE LAW OF HUMAN CONSCIENCE

The creation of the physical universe described in Genesis shows God's framework of created matter coming under certain laws of uniformity and balance that we interpret as laws of nature. These fixed laws were unwritten and left as such for man to discover. However, when God created the first man and woman and placed them in Eden another kind of law was imposed—one of permission and prohibition; both carried rewards and punishments. God moved from unwritten, fixed laws that sustained nature, life, and the universe to spoken, immutable laws that would govern human behavior and the family institution: the law of choice, that of living in a perfect state of fellowship with Him, enjoying the fruit of the tree of life, or choosing to be enlightened with a knowledge of good and evil. Man would choose the fruit of the tree of knowledge of good and evil, which would set the human race on a collision course with itself.

Man's action on his freedom of choice in disobeying God opened the door for God's spoken law to be enforced with punitive measures. The judicial response was swift and complete. Adam and Eve lost the Garden and their perfect status with God, and gained ignoble mortality. It was a lose-lose situation. But in God's court of punitive judgment after man's fall, He introduced another kind of law that would give hope for man's final outcome. It would begin and end with physical pain: Eve, the mother of all living, would be the first to bear the pain of childbirth, and in that pain, motherhood would give birth to a distant second Adam who would reconcile man back to God.

When Adam and Eve were driven from Eden, we see them leaving the Garden with four things: mortality, skins for clothing, a spouse each, and a human conscience. The skins spoke of the future when Israel would be given a courtroom for litigation of sin with animal sacrifices. The tree of knowledge of good and evil also left the Garden as another kind of law inside Adam and Eve in the form of a human conscience. A new age of doom was born: mortality, separation from God, and man's own arbitration over good and evil. The voice of God would no longer speak to man in the cool of the day inside Eden, but in his fallen state, man would hear the voice of God inside his human conscience. Adam and Eve would now be the progenitors of the human race who would carry a conscience knowing right and wrong, required to be acted upon in life, the behavior which would later be judged (Rom. 2:14-15).

The human conscience became an unwritten, permanently fixed law inside Adam and Eve when they departed Eden, and it would serve as God's new rule of law for moral behavior. In the Garden, man had freedom to choose disobedience to God's spoken law. Outside the

Garden, his behavioral acts would be in response to God's voice coming from an inner conscience, making himself the center of his own universe in a court where he would act as judge and jury—a dangerous tightrope to walk. This new inner voice inside fallen man that defined good and evil would allow the rise and fall of individuals and nations. History would become replete with the record of man's defiance against God's moral law of the human conscience.

The law of conscience carried the freedom to lean into the cool breezes of knowing what was good. This would inspire the natural outcome of developmental community law down through the millennia. Historical records of written law that governed societies with moral values would validate that man was a creation of a moral God, and that moral law came about from an inner knowledge of understanding the difference between good and evil. The advanced civilization of the early Sumerians in the Fertile Crescent was an example of this. In 1901, the Code of Hammurabi was found in a Persian city. The discovery astounded archaeologists everywhere. It was a stone marker dating back to 1790 B.C. with 282 inscribed laws that governed the kingdom of Hammurabi. Some of these laws carried the moral edicts of the Ten Commandments. The documentation of history has shown that man lived in a paradoxical world: he had the sense of knowing what was good and right, would create written laws that governed that body of thought, yet failed over and over to keep the laws he had written.

The human conscience served as legal infrastructure

to make individuals accountable for human behavior, not to be a pathway for the restoration of his fallen spiritual state. God's judicial action for this event awaited the litigation of His promise through the woman when, "The seed of the woman would bruise the head of the Serpent."

THE FIRST MARRIAGE: MONOGAMY

The human conscience was not the only permanent law that left the Garden of Eden with Adam and Eve. Fixed inside God's arrangement of marriage with the first man and woman was the law of monogamy. In all of Adam and Eve's loss, having everything ripped from them, they would leave the Garden as a union. The law of two becoming one survived original sin. Monogamous marriage had been established as a fixed paradigm for man's earth journey and would serve as a model for two marriages yet to come in another dimension. Four millennia after Adam and Eve's departure from Eden, Jesus would use the record as case law to argue God's law of permanence in monogamous unions: "Have you not read...they twain shall be one flesh...What therefore God hath joined together, let not man put asunder" (Matt. 19:4-6 KJV).

Missionaries going beyond the borders of Western culture sometimes find themselves in societies that have strayed from God's rule of monogamy. Some find themselves in communities that permit the institution of polygamy, a condition where a man has more than one wife. Other missionaries, on rare occasions, may find themselves living among people that practice the opposite of polygamy: polyandry. Polyandry is a term used to describe a culture's acceptance of women having more than one husband simultaneously, certainly a practice only among a small minority in the world.

The law of monogamy was institutionalized in Eden as part of natural order. Since then, this natural order has been violated, subjugating women to the status of chattel property, and today, wherever polygamy is practiced and legitimized, we see its negative downside. When my wife and I were young missionaries, we served in a land where polygamy was practiced, and before converts were baptized in water, they were required to enroll in a class covering the topic of water baptism. Even being a new missionary, I was well prepared to teach and address any question that might arise, and sure enough, the question of polygamy came up. In a class session, one of the astute members asked: "Why is it wrong to have more than one wife when Jacob, David, and others in the Old Testament had multiple wives?" My response could have included a long dissertation on women's equal rights, and the sociological and emotional benefits of monogamy, but as one who held the more erudite answer, I yielded to something the Holy Spirit dropped inside: it was a question in response to a question. I asked, "How many women did God create for Adam?" A pin-drop blanket of quietness fell over the class. We learned that the biblical creation story of two opposite genders in marriage was a permanently fixed law, irrevocable, and that physical and emotional fidelity in the union of two becoming one acted as glue that optimized social and emotional health. We would also learn that the monogamous union of Adam and Eve in the Garden of Eden would become the central theme for the human race that would cast a long shadow over history for two future marriages of another dimension: Israel's marriage to God and Christ's engagement to a special bride, known as the church.

THE SECOND MARRIAGE

God took the two fixed laws of monogamy and conscience, tied them together as a package and used them as tools in His journey with man for his Edenic restoration. He had made a wife for Adam from one of his ribs, a picture of what was to come. Now, He needed a wife for Himself to produce the promised Seed of the woman. He looked toward the future:

> There appeared a great wonder in heaven—a woman
> clothed with the sun, and the moon under her feet, and
> upon her head a crown of twelve stars. And she, being
> with child, cried, travailing in birth, and pained to be
> delivered....And she brought forth a man child, who was
> to rule all nations with a rod of iron: and her child was
> caught up unto God and to his throne. (Rev. 12:1,2,5 KJV)

Events in the Bible that are marked with God's judicial actions carry permanence. His first action gesture in acquiring a wife to fulfill His promise of the coming Seed of the woman starts with His courting Abraham, the patriarch. Akin to our traditional Western custom of wife finding, the courting takes place preliminary to the marriage itself. God's visitations with Abraham show a marriage proposal with specific dowry promises of geography and prolific posterity. In response to God's proposal, Abraham accepts the offer, believes God, and moves to the Promised Land.

A long engagement after a proposed marriage can prove to be a positive thing before the event of a legal ceremony. In God's order of design, it proved to be so. Over 400 years after the dowry promise of geography and prolific offspring to Abraham, Israel, his seed, was pushed through the birth canal of the Red Sea, coughed up on the sands of the desert to be formed and shaped with a written binding marriage contract.

One of God's greatest acts of communication with man on earth after He spoke with Adam and Eve in the Garden was at the Mount Sinai event. His voice would reappear, not in the cool Garden, but on the hot sands of a desert accompanied with a set of laws giving legal entitlement to a monogamous marriage union, written and signed by His own finger, followed by the legalese in the addendums of rules and regulations governing this union. As part of the agreed matrimony, He would choose to live with His wife in the Tabernacle of worship.

Israel, the sand people of Abraham, was birthed as a nation at Mount Sinai and affirmed as such with the infrastructure of civil and religious laws that would govern her people. The centerpiece of her religious life included the tabernacle, the place of worship where God would dwell. The legal arrangement promised to Abraham had been finalized: God had married Israel in covenant form to impregnate her as a people for a promised Seed.

The birth of Israel as a nation was founded on written law: "And he gave unto Moses two tables of testimony, tables of stone, written with the finger of God" (Ex. 31:18 KJV). The judicial uniqueness of the human conscience inside man when he left the Garden of Eden now gave expression in written law, and by writing the commandments in His own penmanship God told the story of permanence and perpetuity of this marriage union between Him and Israel. During Moses' time at Sinai, he would receive voluminous laws governing the civic and religious life of Israel, but there would be only ten laws written directly by God's finger. All further instructions of civic and religious ordinances were transcribed by Moses. The ten laws on the tablets of stone were in a special category. The act of God in creating a second set of commandments, after Moses broke the first set, shows the permanence of God's rule of law.

The Ten Commandments contained laws that revealed who God was and carried the testimony of the created conscience. Whereas formerly unwritten laws of the conscience were the pathways for moral behavior, the written law in stone elevated the judicial accountability of man. Now, man became responsible for two law-standards that would never be abrogated: the law of conscience that man chose in the Garden and the law written in stone, the latter taking precedence over the former.

The judicial nature of God continued on the backside of the desert when He introduced to Moses and the people of Israel a broader picture of His courtroom justice. There in the barren desert, the skins with which He covered Adam and Eve at the time they departed Eden were reintroduced as another kind of covering: judicial clothing by the act of taking animal life as a sacrifice at the tabernacle altar. This juridical court scene was where the guilt of violators was covered until the perfect sacrifice would be made. The redress of the accused would be found only by taking the initiative to appear in the court of the guilty in front of the brazen altar with a live animal sacrifice. This act complied with God's only law of justice: an animal's life in exchange for a covering that would serve as a temporary reprieve until the perfect sacrifice was made for permanent expiation of guilt. The desert scene where written law was given imposed judicial guilt for man with the provision of adjudication of that guilt at the altar with a sacrifice. For the Jew, a new court had been created, a higher court than that of the human conscience.

Israel was now covenanted with God as a national entity, a bona fide wife whose engagement before marriage reached back to the promises made to Abraham. In this covenant arrangement with Israel, the rule of monogamy between God and Israel was put in writing with the first two commandments: "Thou shalt have no other gods before me...Thou shalt not make unto thee any graven image..." (Ex. 20:3-4). God goes on written record in His marriage contract with Israel that He will not tolerate the practice of bigamy.

From the desert scene at Sinai to the time of Jerusalem's defeat by Nebuchadnezzar, a period of about 900 years, Israel's monogamous union with God shows a disheartening and disconcerting record. It reads like a thousand modern tabloids, filled with descriptive liaisons with all the ancient pagan deities of her day. History shows her generational systemic addiction to bigamous unions in violation of the legal order of the first two commandments given at Sinai. God's law of monogamy pushes Him close to abrogating His relationship to Israel, but His mercy yields to punitive and restorative measures:

> I remember the devotion of your youth, how as a wife you loved me and followed me through the desert....But you have lived as a prostitute with many lovers...."Return faithless people" declares the Lord, "for I am your husband." (Jer. 2:2; 3:1, 14 NIV)

God's forgiveness and rehabilitative efforts with the final stroke of the Babylonian captivity restores monogamy as His marriage standard with his people Israel. The years following the return from Babylon to the land of promise set the stage for the epic event of this union's long turbulent journey. With God's intervention, mercy, and care she will carry to full term the promised Fetus: "When the fullness of time was come, God sent forth his Son, made of a woman" (Gal. 4:4 KJV).

THE THIRD MARRIAGE

> This is the covenant I will make with the house of Israel— I will put my law in their minds and write it on their hearts. (Jer. 31:33 NIV)

In the Scriptures, sometimes the end of the story is told at the beginning. When God clothed Adam and Eve with the skins of animals to cover their naked conscience, He was revealing what was to come in the future when there would be a temporary covering for sins. And when He gave Moses detailed building instructions of a worship center on the desert of Sinai that required animal sacrifice as its ultimate purpose, He reached further into the future for the final climax of another marriage by giving the story symbolic meaning, a picture of another order that would restore man to his lost paradise. It would be the final act of His pen, not on tablets of stone, but with the scene of a brazen altar at Calvary speaking words of love and compassion with an appeal to the human heart. The third marriage was all about God writing a new law, not on a tablet of stone, but on the tablet of the human heart. Calvary would be the writing pen and love its ink, a love that would spawn affection in the espoused that would govern the human heart all the way to the Roman coliseum to face the lions.

The law of love in the monogamous espoused union between Christ and the church was elevated to a higher standard than the second marriage at Sinai where law stood alone. An inquirer came to Jesus and asked, "What must I do to inherit eternal life?" The Lord's reply was: "What saith the law?" Israel was married to God through the law. Later, Jesus would say to His disciples, "If you love me—keep my commandments." Real love in an espousal relationship elicits fidelity based on the intrinsic value of love. The creation of Adam and the first woman show a broader picture when the record is placed alongside Calvary:

> And the Lord God caused a deep sleep to fall upon Adam, and he slept: and he took one of his ribs, and closed up the flesh....And the rib, which the Lord God had taken from man, made he a woman, and brought her unto the man. (Gen. 2:21,22 KJV)

The first Adam gave a rib; the second Adam gave His life. Both resulted in the creation of a woman for a marriage union. The difference between the two women was that the latter had to be created because of the failure of the first. Calvary was the deep sleep, the dowry price for the woman of this third marriage, and it commenced the first stage of God making all things new (Rev. 21:5). There would be a new birth, a new creation of a people into a mystical union with God's Son. She would be a bride who would bear the mark of fidelity and commitment—white robes washed in His blood. Having become betrothed, she would wait for the finality of newness: a new body, a new heaven, earth, and a New Jerusalem. The last and final marriage was all about God's work-order of newness. John, the Apostle, hears and sees that finality in the Revelation:

> For the wedding of the Lamb has come, and his bride has made herself ready....I saw the holy city, the new Jerusalem, coming down out of heaven from God, prepared as a bride beautifully dressed for her husband. (Rev. 19:7; 21:2 NIV)

When Adam and Eve left the Garden, they were fallen creatures of the highest order, but carried within was a mysterious creation that would be passed on to the human race, the creation of love and the ability to bond that love with someone of the opposite gender. This love that could only be derived and experienced in a close marriage union was a snapshot of what was to follow between the Person of Calvary and His elect:

> For you know that it was not with perishable things such as silver or gold that you were redeemed...but with the precious blood of Christ, a lamb without blemish or defect. (1 Peter 1:18-19 NIV)

True love is the pen that writes on the heart, not on

the pre-nuptial agreement. As flawed as modern marriage is, it still carries the veracity of the highest order of love in the human dimension by those who make the institution work, and it projects the radiant truth of the love between Christ and the church.

The legal arrangement for the third marriage has been finalized by the payment of Calvary, and the espoused, though still living at home on earth, waits for the bridegroom to arrive to take her to His Father's dwelling:

> I go to prepare a place for you. And if I go and prepare a place for you, I will come again, and receive you unto myself; that where I am you may be also. (John 14:2-4 KJV)

Chapter 9

The Modern Church Ethos

Words, like people, have interesting histories. A word can start out with one meaning in its origin, but arrive at a later time with a changed definition. One of these interestingly changed words that come to us from history is "pinchbeck."

Christopher Pinchbeck (1670-1732) was a well-known clockmaker and toymaker who lived in London. He invented the gold-colored alloy of copper and zinc for making imitation gold watches. Up to the time of his newly invented metal, anyone who wanted a gold watch had to buy a real gold watch. After the discovery of this new metal, consumers found that they could pay much less for a watch that still looked like real gold. The name Pinchbeck took on broad notoriety, and from that time on jewelry that was made out of his newly invented metal came to be known as pinchbeck gold. It also carried another meaning of something a little more sinister: plain old counterfeit.

It's the first definition that's interesting, the one about imitation gold-looking jewelry. Until reading this, some of us did not know we were buying pinchbeck fashionable ornaments when we laid our money down for our gold-looking purchases. Now, we can all upgrade the value of our gold-appearing jewelry inventory by just calling it pinchbeck gold instead of imitation gold.Pinchbeck sounds more sophisticated and carries the feel of it being more valuable than it actually is. Words do play an important role in impressing others, especially, if the "others" don't know the meaning of pinchbeck. It certainly sounds better than imitation or gold-colored. However, when we try to impress friends using the term pinchbeck, we may run the risk of devaluing our jewelry in the minds of others because the word also carries the definition "counterfeit."

Actually, when Christopher Pinchbeck invented the new gold-looking metal, he gave the economy a boost in the watch-making industry. It allowed the masses to buy gold-looking watches they couldn't afford otherwise, and as long as people saw the newly purchased watches from a distance, they wouldn't know the difference between what was imitation and the real thing. The low cost pinchbeck jewelry products gave an overnight element of glitter that could be added to one's "lares and penates" (household treasures) that were not there before. It gave a new bright look to more of the common people. It was a new day for the dazzle of jewelry for the regular folk. Mass production was underway.

Today, when we stand in the crowd to view the marching cavalcade of the Christian religion in the West, we see the resurgence of the pinchbeck enterprise of a different order. As it was in Pinchbeck's time, in our age of technology and affluence there are new inventions that dress up religious America to meet the consumer demands that are out there, some of it innocent and glaring, and some destructive to the soul. The masses love the glitter that decorates religious Americana, and those who love the glitter are pushing their way to the front of the line to buy the bargains that satisfy the taste for the pinchbeck look: cheap, inexpensive and easily changeable.

In an age of religious sparkle in our country, it is important to know the difference between pinchbeck and real gold. Herein lies the problem. When pinchbeck gold in our religious culture is passed off as real, we enter an imitation of the biblical world. Most of us enjoy reading a good novel of interest, and when it's finished, we go on with life knowing the story isn't true even though we may have identified with the writer's narrative and perhaps some of the characters. Generally, most people know the difference between the real and the made-up, that it is innocent to be lost for a short time in an intriguing make-believe realm that has reality connections. However, a few are so moved by a story that they re-read the book several times as if they themselves are part of the tale. There are two possible reasons for this: the writer is exceptionally good, and the story is well written, or the reader has an emotional need to identify with someone in the novel. In this scenario, it's usually the latter. Focus on glitter that excites the senses without a check on reality can cause one to submit to a false reality—a dangerous formula for personal growth and objectivity.

Consumers of religious pinchbeck gold are out in full force. In the modern age of religious sparkle, people are leaning into those cool breezes of glitter without substance and value. It is the broad road that leads to self-ruin, and it is paved with pinchbeck gold. Unlike traditional America, our present environment teaches us to *feel* good more than it gives instruction to *be* good. It is all about ourselves, how we feel, and what we want. Our generation lives in an instant gratification bubble, and if we have to wait for anything pleasurable, we become victims.

This all-about-ourselves lifestyle has become part of the pinchbeck glitter embellishment in much of American religious culture. The age of megachurches and television ministries built around personalities shows off the glitter that size, success, and money are the symbols of God's prosperity and blessings. In this maze of glare, individuals without faces give their resources to empower others to keep the shine glowing. Even homilies are more about us than about God within us. Some can quote more phrases from Christian books on the market than passages from the Bible. From the pulpit, we find life's issues dealt with from marketed books combined with philosophical thought rather than the primary sources of the Scriptures, sermons more around self-improvement themes than theology from the Bible. Americans today are going to church, feeling more, and thinking less. It seems the in-depth preaching of expository sermons is almost passé with our packaged programs of quick-order and instant sermons. Unlike the sermons of the past that were prepared for congregations that had little, today they are created for those who have much and want more and come with a theology tailored to fit that demand.

The Christian religion in America is unique unto itself. Its vibrancy is in a country of innovative extremes, a country filled with ethnic and cultural diversity matched only by its religious diversity. One of our great strengths as a new country is that we accept change, new ideas, and new ways of doing things. The other side of this coin is that we tend to forget our past and traditions that act as anchors in this state of euphoric change.

The pinchbeck culture of change and newness, for the sake of glitter alone, influences a tilt in the direction of what we want, rather than what we need. The culture of newness and change are the keywords. Everything in the church that is bigger and newer is better. Every older generation goes on record about how much better things used to be—the nostalgia of the past. Today, however, the older generation may have a substantive argument against trends of change within the church that run counter to certain traditions. In some places of worship in our new generation, hymns are sung periodically as if to commemorate the history of the church, as if it's time to take a stroll through the church archives so as not to forget the past.

Pinchbeck gold excites emotions; real gold gives somber and reflective meaning to the value of the written Word. Heirlooms containing real gold always possess two things: worth and sentiment. This is a good balance for our religious culture. Lacking these two qualities, the culture of religious music will lose its impact on the next generation. The older generation wants to feel what they sing, but not with cheap glitter. They want their feeling to be borne out of theological thought that gives a meaningful emotional experience. It isn't change that frightens them—it's what's left behind in the process.

The Russians have a national game called chess; the Chinese have their counterpart called xianggi. Americans play their favorite pastime too—it's called television. The glitter of technology that shapes the secular world has an overlapping influence on the religious culture in America. Many young people and adults in the church can cite the names of television programs, movies and celebrities as if they are members of their own family but can't name the first five books of the Bible. Speaking of the Bible, it is rarely carried to church worship now a days; everything one needs is already on the overhead screen, even the pastor's outlined sermon. These are wonderful inventions that make life easier on Sunday mornings by allowing the worshiper to be hands-free. We no longer have to handle the hymnal or hold the Bible. Something seems to be wrong with this picture. Whatever happened to the old Montessori method of tactile learning, reinforced learning by physical touching, like holding a Bible and looking up Scripture references and turning the pages of the old hymnal. Now, that's real old-fashion Montessori learning in the pew! Even the Lord reminds us a little of that tactile learning when we touch and taste the bread and wine from the cup of His body and the feeling that comes from the water by following Him in baptism. The electronic age simplifies our lives, and at the same time makes us lethargic in the exercise of worship, and it may
have impaired our ability to retain what we see and hear.

Glitter has always been around in one form or another, and every new generation has its own new unique shine. Sometimes, though, it can border on personality cults. Even in the New Testament age, Paul said to the church at Corinth, "Every one of you saith, I am of Paul; or I, of Apollos; or I, of Cephas" (1 Cor. 1:12 KJV). The human tendency is to polish the brass found on the person liked the most or the person who can do the most for us. Everyone has a little brass somewhere, and if you can't find it yourself, there's always someone who can. The real weakness in the religious sector is when the public wants glitter, the religious sources are sometimes willing to provide it. It follows the old adage in Hollywood, "Give the public what they want." The modern voices outside the religious gates of glitter are chanting, "Give us a king to rule over us." The urge to polish the brass in human personalities is as old as history, and it is only the strong who refuse the temptation. Paul and Barnabas found that out at Lystra when they refused the polishing exercise of the Lycaonians. After the healing of the lame man, the Lycaonians wanted to offer sacrifices to them as gods; when Paul refused, he was stoned and left for dead.

It is always amazing how certain fish will strike a shiny spinning object in water; anglers call it a lure. It's not difficult to understand fish biting a hook with real bait on it, but a lure! Yes, it's true; we've all been tempted to go after the real bait with a hook at least once in our lifetime. But just to go after a flashing object should give one a pause to consider that God made us a little higher on the cognitive scale than the fish that lunges for spinning brass.

One might wonder if the small, handheld clay lamps that the five virgins used while waiting for the bridegroom without sufficient oil had any pinchbeck gold on them. Could it be that the lack of oil in their lamps was because they were more interested in the way the lamp looked on the outside rather than what was going on inside? Were the lamps decorated with pinchbeck gold and used as ornaments for display, rather than something with which to see? There's nothing wrong with a little diversity in a group of ladies attending a customary wedding function with lamps that glitter, but not having enough oil to go with the rest of the group can prove embarrassing. Perhaps the attention given to the lamps' shiny exterior distracted them from keeping the oil level up where it should have been. It seems the lesson to learn from this is that it's better to have an old, well-used clay lamp filled with oil that will provide long-term light, than one that glitters on the outside with false gold, but empty of oil.

The seventh church of Laodicea in the book of Revelation gives a broad picture of world Christendom. She represents that part of the church that carries lamps without oil. There is no commitment to the purpose of the lamp. She professes—but fails to possess—wants to belong in name but has grown lukewarm. The oil is depleted, yet she still holds the small lamp, well-endowed with affluence, but its glitter comes from a form of pinchbeck gold—it's not real because it lacks oil. She has a good sparkling façade for the public to see—wealth, prestige, and acceptance, but is in a state of complacency; her love has grown lukewarm and indifferent—having a form of godliness, but denying the power. Her dalliances in political correctness, doctrinal impurity, and syncretistic causes make her less than real gold. The union with her espoused has devolved into the false glitter of this world with no energy left in the lamp to provide light. Her heart is empty and sterile of any heartthrob love toward her espoused; she has become unfaithful, having taken on the god of this world. She shows a good façade, but underneath she is emaciated, poor, blind, and naked and is reminded that real gold comes from Him: "I counsel thee to buy of me, gold tried in the fire, that thou mayest be rich" (Rev. 3:18 KJV). She has yielded to the glitter of false gold.

Christopher Pinchbeck passed on to us a new word and did more than invent the pinchbeck gold alloy that increased watch sales: he produced a family of quality watchmakers. Buckingham Palace today houses one of his son's astronomical clocks given to King George III. For decades, his new gold-looking metal created higher sales of watches than before, but the reason they were purchased by the public was not because of what they looked like on the outside; it was the quality of the internal working parts. The cheap glitter on the outside was attractive, but a watch that kept accurate time on the inside was better. David said, "Thou desireth truth on the inward parts." Today, it is the people who look beyond the glitter who will find lasting value in their walk of faith. They will measure life beyond the substance of the package something comes in. Pinchbeck gold is never passed on as an heirloom, and in God's economy, if the inner part keeps accurate time, the outside is always real gold.

The false and real gold have lived side-by-side, like the wheat and tares in Jesus' parable, and today, the grain has ripened and is ready for harvest. Separation of the real from the false is inevitable, and the church, Adam's rib, can be seen trimming her lamp making herself ready for the marriage celebration.

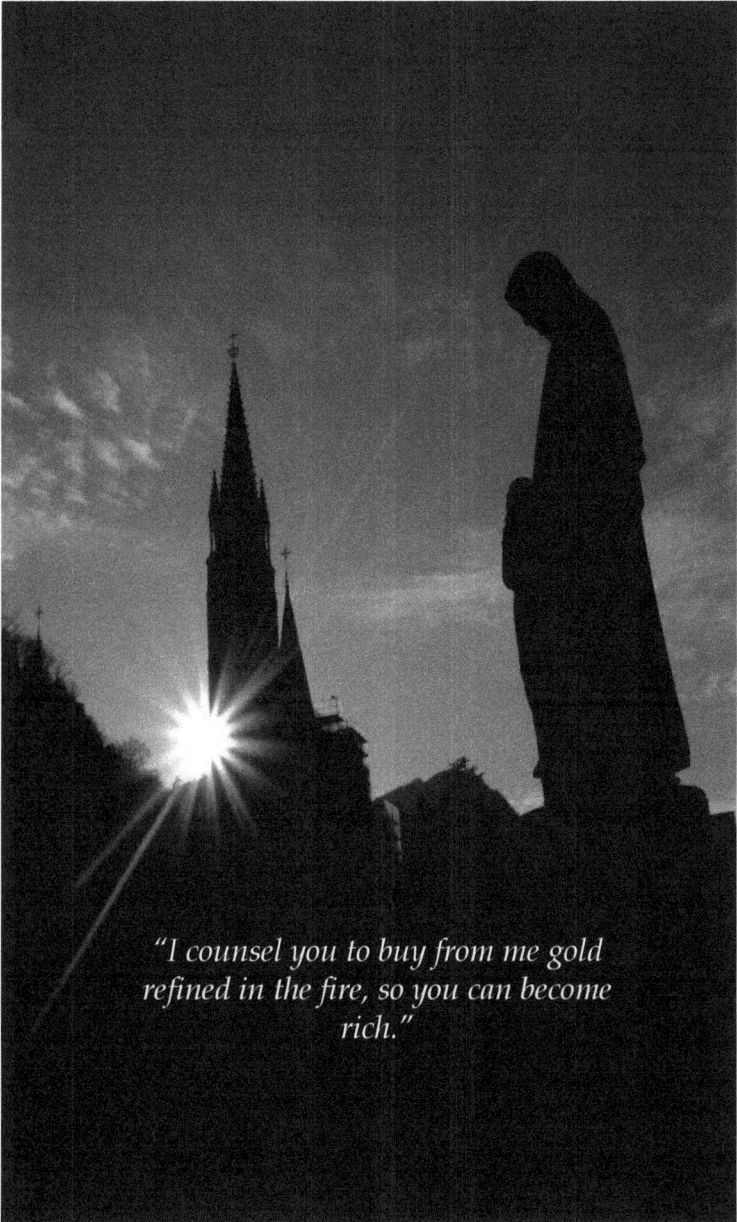

"I counsel you to buy from me gold
refined in the fire, so you can become
rich."